FAITH IN EDUC

CW01642881

Also by Thomas FitzPatrick

Catholic Secondary Education in South-West Scotland before 1972: Its Contribution to the Change in Status of the Catholic Community of the Area (1986)

The Parish of Holy Cross, Glasgow 1886–1986 (1986)

Weather and War (1992)

No Mean Service (1995)

Thomas FitzPatrick

FAITH IN EDUCATION

THE TEACHER AS WITNESS

To Charles Kennedy
with thanks

Thomas A. FitzPatrick

17/09/09

MUNGO

Published in the United Kingdom by

MUNGO BOOKS
An imprint of Ovada Books

Saint Mungo's Retreat, 52 Parson Street
Glasgow, G4 0RX

Tel/Fax +44 (0)141 552 5523

www.mungo.ovadabooks.com
info@ovadabooks.com

ISBN 978-1-905965-07-6

© Thomas FitzPatrick 2009

Database right Ovada Books (maker)
All rights reserved

David Higham Associates Ltd, 5–8 Lower John Street, Golden Square, London, W1R 4HA for 'The Star-gazer' by Louis MacNeice. Reprinted by permission

Saint Michael's College, Toronto, for the passage from *The Terrors of the Year 2000* by Étienne Gilson. Reprinted by permission

British Cataloguing in Publication Data. A catalogue record for this book is available from the British Library

Digitally printed in Glasgow by Bell & Bain Ltd
www.bell-bain.com
∞

Dedicated to the Reverend W. E. Brown, D. D., M. C.

Chaplain to Catholic students, Glasgow University, 1929–1945

I acknowledge, with pleasure and thanks, the illumination received in encounters with pupils, students, teachers, colleagues, mentors, and friends over many years, and recently with the publishers. All contributed positively to this study. Its errors and deficiencies are mine.

Contents

Introduction

The title, *Faith in Education* prompts two questions: what is Education and what is Faith?

Education comes about in a multitude of ways. For our present purpose, the word is used in a limited sense, to mean the formal education provided in the state system by teachers licensed to do so.

Faith can be used in two ways: to mean either a strong belief in something with or without proof or a specific system of religious or quasi-religious belief. According to dictionaries, both are acceptable. Both seem to say, somewhat confusingly, that faith is faith. Whatever it is, we live by it.

The title of the work can be read in two ways.

In one, the emphasis is on the term Education. Read thus, it asserts that there is a strong belief in the community at large that education as delivered by a systematic, formal educational system, is 'a good thing', carrying within itself, as it were automatically and by its own nature, the answer to those many questions about the human condition that are raised by the young. The community believes in education to provide these answers.

If read in another way, the emphasis is on the traditions and word Faith. The title then asserts that there is in formal education systems a belief in something, a faith that underpins and sustains it. This reading wishes to focus the attention of the reader on that belief.

The essay itself is a work of faith. Its first article says that the teacher in the classroom, face to face with the pupil, is central to the educational process. It encapsulates a belief that for any educational system to work, its teachers have to have faith in that some thing; be it religious or non-religious, on which the system is based: and that there is no substitute for the teacher, even in a computer-driven society.

The second article is that all educational systems have a basis in a faith of some kind. In some, as for example Catholic, Anglican, Jewish or Islamic systems that faith is a specific system of religious belief. In those that are not so based, as for example a secularist, humanist system, the underpinning something that sustains the system may be a philosophical principle or an ideology. The principle may be explicit or implicit. If such a system is effective in practice, the educational process takes on a religious or quasi-religious nature. This article states the belief that it is not possible to provide an education without some supportive faith. All schools are, *au fond*, faith schools. Only the gods are different.

The third article is a belief that the success of any system depends on the commitment of its teachers to the fundamental premise on which the system is founded. That is, success in education depends on the faith of the teachers who deliver it as well as on the faith on which the system is based. Success is known by the fruits.

The fourth article is the belief that education in western civilisation was underpinned by Christian faith and values, and was in practice the business of the churches. When in the modern era the concept of 'free and compulsory' education for all took root, the upbringing of the rising generations was gradually taken over by civil authority. With the decline of adherence to the mainstream churches and the alienation from them of the rising generations, a philosophical and spiritual vacuum developed at the heart of the educational process, manifested particularly in the area of moral education. Nevertheless governments, politicians, parents and citizens generally still have faith in education, and all of them expect teachers to provide it. This work attempts to examine the 'existential' situation of the teacher who is called upon to provide this elixir, or panacea called education.

The fifth article holds that education has to be delivered with authority if it is to be effective, and that the natural source of authority over a child is its parents.

The sixth article says that education has a moral dimension. Because education is conducted in a social milieu, and is concerned with human relations, all education is *de facto* moral education. In a system based on a specific religion, moral education is presented within that framework. Where a system is not so based, this work believes that the system has to find some principle or ideology on which to base its moral teaching, and believes that in practice it will come to be of a religious or quasi-religious nature.

Young people ask searching questions about the world around them. The seventh article states the belief that teachers have to acquire an overall view of the universe that will satisfy the demands of their pupils and also be consistent with the faith they themselves hold and are trying to teach. For their teaching to be effective, teachers have to be faithful witnesses to their belief whatever it may be, and able to justify it to themselves as well as to their pupils.

The seventh article states that something of the ancient Christian pedagogical tradition survives within the educational system, even in parts that are not specifically religious. It believes that the tradition is sustained mainly by the faith and practice of teachers, and that to preserve what remains of it, some knowledge of its historical development is necessary.

The eighth article believes that education should lead to

the harmonious and integrated development of persons at home with themselves and the universe, and to a unity of spirit in the community. It believes that this cannot be achieved without a unifying belief in the nature of the universe and of the place of humankind in it.

The ninth article believes that this unifying faith is belief in the existence of God. This belief accords with the vision expressed in Gilson's prophetic prose-poem, *The Terrors of the Year 2000*, which foresees the state of a world without faith in anything but human intelligence, wisdom and energy.

The tenth article says that faith by itself is not sufficient. There must also be hope and charity.

God is Love.

1

Faith in Education
The Teacher as Witness

Every educational system has a moral goal that it tries to attain and that informs its curriculum.

Alan Bloom, *The Closing of the American Mind*

Whatever the problem, be it a matter of road safety, dependence on drugs, inculcating habits of thrift, obesity, or improving the national sporting performance, there is a faith which holds that education can provide the remedy.

It is a faith that could move such molehills. Could it move mountains? In a culturally divided nation, is it the unifying force that could bind diverse communities together?

An even more serious question arises. If the problem to be addressed happens to arise from a weakness or deficiency in education itself, where are we to go for the cure? Can that physician cure himself? Or, should it be herself?

From where does this faith in education originate? For centuries before the Education Act of 1696, and for three hundred years after it, an educational system, founded on Christian principles shaped the life of this nation. The extraordinary material and cultural progress of Scotland after the Union of Parliaments in 1707 was above all attributable to the standards of Scottish education.[1]

By the end of the second millenium of the Christian Era the system appeared to be working well. The proportion of the population attaining to secondary, or higher levels was steadily increasing; the needs of the deaf, the blind, or those with other special educational requirements were being sympathetically catered for; the intellectual and practical demands of a complex technological economy were being met, and provision was envisaged for the formal education of the whole population from the pre-school to the university level.

PRESENT DISCONTENT

Nevertheless, there was an awareness, especially among those closest to the action, the teachers, that all was not well. Although teacher-pupil ratios had greatly improved and material rewards for teachers were greater than they had ever been, teacher morale remained low. On the one hand it was denied that educational standards were falling while on the other there was an insistence that they needed to be raised. Although statistics could be quoted to show that performance at the Leaving Certificate and other comparable examinations was as good if not better than it had ever been, there was evidence of decline in mastery of the written and spoken word. In the general area of modern languages, not only were higher standards being attained in Europe and elsewhere, attainment in Scotland had fallen well below its own former level. References to the leading position that Scotland once held in the field of education, and to the reform needed if that pre-eminence were to be regained, were evidence of the general malaise.

One source of parental and teacher uneasiness lies in the area of morals and manners, rather than in the academic field. If the Assembly at Holyrood needs to reform the present system, as it may have to do, it must needs do so in a very changed social, economic, moral, cultural and spiritual context, and will have to carry through its reforms in a climate of increasing indiscipline in schools, a growing drug culture and an increase in teenage pregnancies, all of which affect children of ever-younger age groups. It will have to do this without the support of the ancient certainties that sustained its seventeenth century predecessor. In the past, the community's moral goals and objectives were generally accepted, and teachers were aware of the thrust of the educational system in the area of moral education, and of their part in sustaining it. In this age not only has this consensus diminished, the goal posts have been moved without the main players having been notified.

EDUCATION ACT 1945

The root causes of the present discontent have to be sought in the changes in society's manners and mores since the end of the Second World War and in the reaction of the educational system to those changes. The Education Act of 1945 initiated a far-reaching, often agonising and still ongoing revolution, in which the accepted functions and objectives of education, particularly at secondary level, were subjected to a fierce reappraisal, carried out in the light of two fundamental principles: one, that it is a natural right of all children of whatever ability or social status to an education that will allow him or her to develop to his or her fullest potential; and two, that a liberal state will quite properly seek to ensure, through education, that the creative energies of a new generation are used to direct the forces of change along lines which are socially desirable and in general accord with the nation's traditions and practices.[2]

Contained in these principles were assumptions about the nature of secondary education, about the role of the school and its power to influence the lives of pupils and the society in which they lived, and about the priority of the rights of the educators over those of the parents and of the children themselves. There is an assumption also of a consistency between the principles themselves, yet within them are concealed those conflicting forces which tend to polarise all educational effort, towards the development of the individual person on the one hand and on meeting the needs of the community on the other. Finally, there is an assumption that there is a 'general accord' with the nation's traditions and practices, and that these are clear and unchanging. It is our belief that the faith on which educational tradition was based was Christianity. Can it still be said that there is a general accord with that view? Even if there is, can it be assumed that that accord will be maintained in the secular and multi-religious society that is emerging?

In the application of these principles a series of substantial changes in the system was introduced, in every instance by government decree. These were followed in rapid succssion by short-term measures that were needed to clear up the problems that resulted from these changes. The untimely raising of the school leaving age, first to fifteen and then to sixteen, at the time when the post-World War II 'baby boom' was about to reach the schools, led inevitably to a shortage of teachers, which had to be countered by dilution of professional standards. In the 1960s a philosophical *non sequitur*, that equality of esteem of persons requires that all be treated identically, began to be given expression in educational practice. Man, or Woman, the adult, ceased to be the measure of all things, and was replaced by the child, especially the female child.

Hand in hand with this misunderstanding of equality went Milton's nymph, sweet Liberty.[3] For example, in the introduction of guidance systems it was suggested that children should be free to work out their own code of behaviour and moral salvation, without any reference to centuries of human experience.[4] When in the 1970s it was assumed that everyone had the potential to graduate at university level, the situation envisaged by Gilbert's Don

Alhambra in *The Gondoliers* was in sight: 'Lord Chancellors were cheap as sprats, and Bishops in their shovel hats were plentiful as tabby cats … and Party Leaders you might meet in twos and threes in every street'. At every stage it was the lot of a dedicated, over-worked and perhaps too compliant teaching profession to face the impositions of government, and try to make them work.

Faith in education in its origin had its foundation in religious faith. With the advance of scientific knowledge and decline of religious practice and belief, this foundation has been eroded, and a new faith, faith in education has taken its place. Curiously, in a period when uncertainty has been elevated to the status of a philosophical principle, this faith bucks that trend by holding with remarkable certainty that the pursuit of knowledge of whatever kind will by itself bring about a prosperous and harmonious society.

The axioms of this new faith are: Education (undefined) in itself is a good thing. Therefore it is right to compel children to be educated. Moral development can be achieved without reference to any basis in religious belief. Science is a law unto itself. The function of the teacher is to impart knowledge and instil attitudes in line with the fiat of a superior authority.

SOME AIMS OF EDUCATION

Statements about the aims of education have never been in short supply. As for example:

> The desirable outcome of our educational system … is well-adjusted children equipped for adulthood and work, with a body of knowledge and an ability to think for themselves.[5]

> The ultimate purpose … is the transmission of values and ideas.[6]

> Ideally, the educational experience of an individual should lead

to his harmonious and integrated development, and result in a person in command of himself and at peace with the universe.[7]

And the establishment view:

[The ultimate aim of education is to] promote the spiritual, moral, cultural, mental and physical development of pupils and of society, and prepare them for the opportunities and experiences of adult life.[8]

Beguiling as these dicta are, what they really express is an unbounded faith in education. Nor does any one of them give any indication of how its objectives are to be achieved, nor of who may be the gods and goddesses willing and able to carry through the awesome tasks outlined.

FAITH NEEDS HOPE – AND CHARITY

With this faith in education goes hope – hope that somehow all will be well. The time-honoured principle of 'muddling through' is not satisfactory in education, nor anywhere else. Likewise, faith without good works will not suffice to promote the spiritual, moral, cultural, mental and physical development of the rising generations. From where can we expect the good works to come? It is surely axiomatic, even in an age dominated by electronic communication, that an educational system requires teachers to make it happen; and further, that a successful outcome will depend on their devotion to the cause. For education, education, education, read teachers, teachers, teachers.

Serious questions have to be addressed. Was there a generally accepted moral objective that the educational service used to seek to attain? Was it pursued solely by the educational system? Does such an objective exist now? If so, does it differ substantially from the traditional aim? If it does, should the former objective be restored?

In the past the moral objective of the system was a derivative of the Christian gospel, which gave it its goals and informed the curriculum. In the light of the decline in adherence to the mainstream churches, is the restoration of the former moral goals possible? If it were to be attempted, would this be a task for the educational service alone? Is there an alternative source of moral direction in sight? Who should decide in issues of this nature? The Scottish Parliament? Should teachers have a positive input into the decision-making process in matters of morals, or is it their function simply to carry out instructions handed down from on high? In such a case, where education becomes indoctrination, would it be possible to provide a truly liberal education? Is there a hidden curriculum developing within the Scottish system that seeks to fill the vacuum left by the decline of formal religion? Can a moral education be provided without a religious basis? Is secularism in fact an alternative religion? The great civilisations of the past were sustained by educational systems with a basis in religion, and the same could be said of some modern secular societies such as Nazi Germany, Soviet Russia, or western capitalism. Only the gods were different.

European civilisation, from which our educational tradition springs, was nourished at least from Charlemagne's time by educational systems based on Christian values, in which morality and religious faith were intertwined. In the modern era a creeping secularism has eroded that ancient tradition.[9] By the end of the second millenium a mindset had developed in which it became more and more difficult to synthesise the truths of science and religion, and a widespread alienation from the mainstream churches resulted, affecting particularly the young. The concepts of authority and discipleship that were rooted in religious belief have been undermined, and as a result the moral authority of parents and teachers and even of government itself are threatened. The notion that Hell, if it does not exist, will have to be re-invented, could be gaining ground.

The vision of the human being which the ancient tradition nurtured is fading. If that vision is to be recaptured, a new synthesis between the spiritual needs of the individual person and the complexities of modern scientific knowledge has to be found.

In the absence of any clear moral objectives, confusion and uncertainty reign. After 1872, when the civil authority took control of national education, the belief gained ground that science, having destroyed faith in biblical revelation, could solve all problems, and the historic link between religion and morality within the educational system began to be eroded. A new, secular, faith grew which assumed that fundamental moralities were natural to humanity and that a code of ethics existed on which all men were agreed, and for which they needed no religion as support. It need hardly be said that this was deeply questioned by the behaviour of allegedly civilised men in the horrific wars of the twentieth century, and most seriously by the Shoah.

FUTURE – IMPERFECT?

The problems that secularisation has spawned have to be confronted, but whether teachers are in a positon to tackle issues of this order is gravely to be doubted. Being for the most part employees of the State they have to accept its aims of instilling literacy, numeracy and other utilitarian knowledge, its curricular constraints and priorities, its concept of authority, and its separation of religious and secular education. They have to encourage pupils to be independent thinkers aspiring to freedom of thought and action, fit to become members of a mature democracy, without enjoying substantial personal and professional freedom themselves.

Those who would uphold the Christian educational tradition have to face the additional problem of reconciling the conflicts, real or imagined, that have arisen between Christian cosmology and modern scientific culture. Their current unease is hardly surprising. And those who look first to the teachers to bring about the moral regeneration that is needed, have to face the further questions, whence comes the teacher's moral and spiritual power to direct others, and ultimately, who will teach the teachers? Formerly teachers accepted their part in the general area of moral education. Now, mutual understanding of the objectives has diminished. Is it being re-established, on a radically different base?

It is held to be axiomatic that the intellectual and spiritual commitment of teachers to whatever educational philosophy they are trying to impart, is a necessary condition of a successful outcome. If by success is meant willing and free acceptance of the philosophy by those taught, then the intellectual and spiritual commitment of the teachers is not sufficient. The teacher's problem is how to gain this acceptance, while respecting the freedom of those taught to accept or reject.

If not the teachers, then, to whom should the community look for a restatement of moral goals? Historically it looked to the Christian churches, in varying ways at different times, for moral guidance as well as a first port of call for material as well as spiritual aid in time of need. The advent of the Welfare State has left the churches struggling to enunciate their relevance in present-day society. This theme was examined at some length by McSweeney, who pointed to an interdependence between the churches and secular society whereby each tends to modify the other.[10] In his view post-Reformation Protestantism spawned capitalism, and then was transformed by it. In divided Christendom the Catholic Church rejected 'the world', and became cut off from other Christian believers, then in the late twentieth century Catholicism was being transformed in its turn. Theology, morality and liturgy began to reflect the characteristics of the secular world, and this resulted in a proliferation of moral and theological dissent. The long-standing decline in commitment to all the mainstream churches increased, and teachers, no longer having the traditional support of Church and Home, have been left to seek their own goals as best they might.

A major source of alienation from the life of the institutional churches, and an additional source of difficulty for educators, is related to the transformation of the view of reality caused by advances in science and technology. Psychology, sociology and genetics have altered the understanding of personality and of human imperfection. Sin has to be understood in the context of limitations imposed by temperament and environment, and the responsibility of individuals for their own behaviour is substantially reduced. The consequences for the teacher are dire. Wrongdoers can no longer be held responsible for their deeds – although strangely enough those who do well expect to be recognised and rewarded. Punishment, corporal or other, becomes morally unjust. The educator has to fall back on a policy of persuasion by rational argument, even although psychological, sociological and genetic understanding have made it clear that reason has its limitations, in the teacher no less than in the pupil. Issues related to evolutionary theory cannot be avoided by teachers at any level or in any subject area. Answers to the great questions of creation and the meaning of life have to be found that are consistent with both religious and scientific truth, that leave the teacher with liberty of conscience and intellectual integrity and that can stand the test of time for pupils.

Parenthetically it has to be noted, however, that the decline in support for the institutional churches has been accompanied by an outpouring of sympathy for humanity in distress, especially among the young. Innumerable charitable enterprises flourish. In the absence of systematic information about the religious beliefs of those outside the churches, it may be a mistake to think of this era as irreligious. A substantial fraction of the population retains private, even secret, religious interpretations which are extraordinarily resilient, the reasons for which have to do with their importance as a source of meaning, a basis for moral behaviour and an ultimate resource in dealing with personal suffering.[11]

The alienation of the younger generations from the mainstream churches, combined with the increase in duration of compulsory attendance at school, throws into prominence the role of the schools in maintaining or preserving the ethical traditions of the nation. It would seem that the preservation of a Christian tradition in the educational system will depend more than ever on the work and stances of individual teachers. Whatever theological tradition they belong to, they share a great deal of common ground, just as they face common problems. Their common ground, expressed in the two great commandments of the Old and New Testaments, is shared also by Jews and Muslims. For a multicultural community to thrive, there is a need to develop a cosmology common to all faiths that can accommodate these conflicts. If the Christian tradition is not to be restored, some other rational foundation for faith in the educational system will have to be found.

2

By What Authority?
The Teacher as Parent

The teacher's authority to direct, discipline or otherwise mould pupils derives from several sources: in its academic aspect, from a university or other appropriate institution; in its professional aspect, including suitability to be in charge of children, from a Faculty of Education or equivalent body; and, in its legal aspect, from Parliament. The freedom of the teacher is further constrained by the requirements of local authorities or other employers, and by a national curriculum cemented by an examination system. Finally, in schools of a denominational character, authority to teach requires the approval of the appropriate religious body.

The problem was faced squarely in post-revolutionary France. The Commission of Public Instruction was set up to supervise all educational establishments, to control qualification for and entry into teaching, and to monitor the content and ethos of the curriculum. A long-running dispute between Church and State ensued, at the centre of which were conflicting views of the source of authority. The Church claimed to have divine authority, on the basis of the gospel command, 'Go ye and teach all nations', whereas the State saw authority to be derived from the democratic will of the people. The latter proposition, which begged the question who or what is 'the state', turned out to be less simple than at first appeared. The democratic view was first ousted when the doctrine of the

Divine Right of the monarchy was replaced by Napoleonic military despotism.[12]

Before the Reformation, the Catholic Church was the principal provider of education in Europe. Even when the unity of Christendom was broken and a theological fault-line opened to divide the continent, education continued to be based on an authority that was religious in nature. The old régime continued to hold sway in the Catholic south, while the Protestant north saw Church and State as two aspects of a related authority in the field of education. The system that emerged was based on Christian faith and values, until the secularisation of the post-Enlightenment era penetrated society, and the dominance of the State in education steadily increased.

There is however another source of the teacher's authority, recognised throughout the ages not only in the Judaeo-Christian tradition but also in ancient Rome and other pagan societies.[13] Parents, who under God are the authors of their children, have a natural duty to protect and cherish them, and a corresponding right to exercise authority over them. Children in their turn have a duty to be disciples of their parents in return for their right of nourishment. Parents have a right and duty to present the model of behaviour that will bring their children willingly to recognise the way of life they believe the children should follow. Children have a right to expect guidance in how to live, and a corresponding duty to respect and honour their parents.

Parental authority, rooted in the nature of things, may be, to some degree, delegated to teachers, and for centuries this was an accepted practice. Formal education was an holistic activity in which responsibilities were shared by Home, Church and School. The authority conferred on the teacher was upheld by a consensus, forged by these agencies, that recognised the rights and limitations of the authority of each. This consensus was at the centre of a system in which intellectual and spiritual life were nourished by an education that reflected Christian ideals and values.

In our age, all three pillars of educational wisdom are under attack. Family life is breaking down, religious belief is declining, and an unparalleled explosion of knowledge and communication technology has radically changed the position of the schools and compounded the difficulties of the teachers. A secularist culture has emerged in which the traditional view of the sanctity of human life has been discarded, masculine and feminine roles are confused and moral uncertainty elevated into a virtue. The ancient religious tradition has been eroded in a multitude of ways, and the current malaise in education and in society at large can be traced to the resultant weakening of the religious and philosophical base. Cultural changes have rendered ever more difficult the problems of unifying the deepest aspirations of young people growing up, and of reconciling the mental sets demanded by the apparently conflicting insights of objective knowledge and subjective experience.[14]

> Today it is more difficult than it once was to synthesise the various disciplines of knowledge and the arts. While the volume and diversity of the elements which make up our culture increase, at the same time the capacity of individual men to perceive them and to blend them organically decreases, so that the image of the universal man becomes ever more faint.[15]

Most significant for the preservation of the traditional Christian ethos of the schools, and also for the mental health of teachers, is the condition of the family, 'the primary sphere of human life where the deepest expressions of fidelity, of trust in other persons, of self-acceptance and of growth in intimacy either does or does not occur'.[16] It is 'the dynamic principle of society and the source of social continuity ... [the family] acquires a distinctively religious character'.[17] The institution of the family is under immense strain, as is evidenced by the prevalence of divorce, the numbers of one-parent families – a misnomer if ever there was one – the widespread acceptance of abortion, and the abuse and abandonment of children on a horrifying scale.[18] This breakdown is accompanied by a decline in the sense of community at every level. Neighbourhoods in essence no longer exist; civic life is fragmenting to the point where politics no longer work. In a society which finds it difficult to accept that real love involves sacrifice, a significant fraction of the rising generation is growing up in a state of moral and intellectual bewilderment.

The family is not an appendage to the school or parish, but the very foundation of both. It has been described as the domestic church, where the central drama of life is enacted and the journey of living faith experienced. Christians, following Christ's teaching and the Judaic tradition, affirm the sacredness of marriage as an irrevocable, lifelong, legal contract between a man and a woman, bestowing on one another conjugal rights and creating a sacramental bond which makes them *two in one flesh*. This fundamental principle ennobles and sanctifies the married state, which derives its strength from the fact that it has its basis *in the nature of things*. It is a pattern for living, a metaphysical reality *cum fundamento in re* which for all the assaults on it refuses to die.

In the education of children there is no substitute for the authority of the family. In the past, in the eyes of the law the teacher stood *in loco parentis*, and the schools could call on parental support to reinforce their demands. When parental authority is eroded, the absence of discipline in the home spills over into the schools, and the authority of the school also weakens. To what extent a teacher can be said to act in place of parents who have abandoned their natural responsibility for their children is far from clear. The status of the teacher is even more confused at the upper levels of the secondary school, where students over sixteen are legally free to enter into the married state. Discussion of 'education' without regard to the consequences of marital breakdown obscures the nature of the problems that have to be addressed, oversimplifies such important issues as the essential difference between primary and secondary education, and overlooks the impact of broken families on the performance of pupil and teacher.

Divorce was the great departure from the Christian ideal of marriage, and its advent has been followed by a further deviation by which cohabitation and marriage are made increasingly convergent concepts in the eyes of the law.

> Divorce ... has been shown to be associated with a wide range of social and psychological difficulties, for both the couple and the children. Cohabitation is no guarantee of marital stability: on the contrary, where there has been cohabitation before a marriage, there is more likeliehood of its breaking down. Christian teaching must always promote the gospel values of monogamy, creativity and responsibility for children.... Young people must be helped to appreciate that monogamy, permanency and fidelity are enabling processes for the sustaining, healing and growth of the couple ... marriage ... within the traditional signposts is a dynamic state.[19]

Modern marriage and traditional marriage have become different things. The former is totally secular, with no apparent roots in religion or for that matter in nature. It is part of a culture that puts its highest premium on private freedom, private choice, private goals, individual rights and individuality. While much of this is healthy, an excessive attachment to privacy helps to make it more difficult to make or sustain permanent commitments or to sacrifice oneself for others.

As with the traditional family, so with the mainstream churches. The long-standing decrease in membership continues. More than sixty per cent of Catholics in the

Archdiocese of Glasgow, who make up almost two-thirds of the Scottish total, do not attend Mass regularly. In Scotland as a whole, only seventeen per cent or thereabouts of the adult population are regular attenders at any church services. Remarkably, in view of their former reputation for religious disputation, Scots now have the poorest record of church attendance of any part of the United Kingdom. 'The Church today is facing an erosion of faith in an atmosphere of secularism, which has found its way into the Church.'[20] This decline is not confined to one church or to one country. Vocations to the ministerial priesthood and to religious life have dwindled throughout the western world. Inevitably with it there goes a decrease in willingness to accept religious authority, and ultimately respect for all authority is eroded, compounding the difficulties facing those charged with the formation and education of the young.

Along with the decline in family life and in Church membership has gone an expansion of the educational system, so vast that it is on longer appropriate to talk in general terms of an institution called 'the school'. Now the formal educational process begins in the nursery, and continues through primary and secondary stages to further, higher and tertiary levels, and beyond. At every stage the function of the teacher appears to be to dispense something called 'education', an elusive concept, which many seem to think is a commodity available on demand. The schools system of the post-Reformation period, backed by the authority of Home and Church, and licensed by the State, was an effective instrument in the spiritual, moral and intellectual formation of the young. It reflected the values and requirements of the society that it served, and in so doing had to devote much effort to utilitarian and vocational aspects. It is probable that the success of the system was due in some measure to the evangelical fervour that was brought to the educational process.

The function of the school, however, was to serve, not to lead. As the values and requirements of society shifted towards utilitarian ends, educational objectives changed. The confidence of the school as a mentor in moral issues has been weakened by the confusion in such matters of society at large, while in the area of secular education its unique position as a purveyor of truth and knowledge has been eroded by a revolution in information technology. Even in the mundane area of commerce and industry, a bewildering rate of change in what is demanded from the schools adds to the uncertainties of teachers. The explosion of knowledge affects churchmen and parents as well as teachers and pupils, affects attitudes to religious belief and moral behaviour, and a weakening of the philosophical basis of education inevitably follows.

If education has to regain something of the moral and intellectual integrity that graced it in the past, its philosophical foundation has to be restored. Such an effort would be in keeping with the spirit of the founding fathers of the modern Scottish system. 'I don't mean to say', said S. S. Laurie, 'that it is necessary that a teacher should be a philosopher, but it is quite indispensible that he should philosophise ... If he does not, he degrades himself.'[21] The problem is to find a suitable *point de départ* for the restoration of the educational edifice, at a time when the love of wisdom is at a discount.

The answer has to be found in reviving what remains of the ancient consensus. Education, like any other form of social activity involving human beings, requires some kind of moral code to control its operation. It is in the acceptance of the need for a moral basis for the educational process that vestiges of the consensus remain, and it could be argued that it is from this general consensus that the authority of the teacher is now derived. Just how strong the consensus is, and how capable of survival is open to doubt. In recent years acts of violence against teachers in the classroom have increased and voices have been heard suggesting that teachers may have to take legal action to defend themselves against allegations made by pupils and parents. Actions in the opposite sense are already part of the educational scene.

In the past the philosophical basis of education reflected the religious beliefs and practices of the nation at large. As adherence to Christian belief declines, the denial of moral absolutes is more and more widespread. Even among Christians themselves the old certainties are disappearing.[22] A basis for consensus has to be found, which will recognise the ultimate source of the authority over pupils, without which an educational system can not function. It may be that the necessary basis will be found in the recognition that parents are the ultimate source of authority over their children. There are signs on the part of some educational authorities to concede something in that direction, by increasing the autonomy of individual schools and allowing parents greater freedom of choice in educational matters.

3

Moral Education
The Teacher as Guide

Every educational system has a moral goal that it tries to attain and that informs its curriculum.

Allan Bloom, *The Closing of the American Mind*

All Education is Moral Education.

That there is a moral dimension in education can be taken as axiomatic: so much so, that the notion that all education is moral education is widely accepted.

There are many parts of the school curriculum that could be regarded as part of moral education; one might claim that moral education in its widest sense is the prime function of the school.[23]

Virtually all subjects of the school curriculum have something to contribute to the personal development of pupils.[24]

Young people should be assisted in the harmonious development of their physical, moral and intellectual endowments [and] encouraged to weigh moral values … and to embrace them by personal choice.[25]

Value judgments are indispensable to the special work of the thinker as they are to any rational life.… Some moral qualities are essential to understanding, and some defects are fatal to it. To cultivate these qualities and to eradicate these defects is … deeply germane to the whole work of education.[26]

One function of the school is to pass on society's moral and social inheritance, and direct the sentiments and habits of young people towards the good life.[27]

All of these statements concur that all education has a moral dimension. The last goes further, expressing a worthy aim, impossible of fulfilment if there is no consensus on what constitutes the good life.

THE NEED FOR A MORAL CODE

Even the most militant of those nineteenth century French anti-clericals who advocated non-religious education in schools, recognised the need for moral education, holding that fundamental moralities are natural to humanity and that a code of ethics could be found on which all men could be agreed.[28] In the absence of a religious basis, the question arises, what code?

Social morality depends on agreed standards, on a consensus which is so universally accepted it hardly needs to be discussed. In the real world of education, the moral dimension is expressed in relationships, between teacher and taught, that have to be forged in a crucible of goal-seeking activities pursued together. A code is required to rule the behaviour of the actors in this drama, which will allow the relationships to flourish and the commonly (*sic*) sought goals to be most readily achieved. It may be arrived at by mutual consent, or imposed unilaterally: the important fact is that it must exist. It will reflect a view, emanating from those who framed it, of the nature of human persons, and also of the value of the goals being pursued. It will be called upon to resolve issues involving the freedom of the pupil and the limits of the authority of the teacher. It will have to have regard for the intellectual and spiritual essence of both pupil and teacher, and must therefore be based on concepts that take account of the total nature of each. It will require agreement in principle between them on the degree of freedom to be accorded to the pupil, the extent of the authority of the teacher, and the nature of the sanctions that may be invoked in the event of failure on the part of either to observe the code.

A GUIDING PRINCIPLE

The respect accorded to the pupil by the teacher and to the teacher by the pupil which the code incorporates, will find its justification in a belief about the nature of persons, just as the respect towards subjects of study will also be founded on some basic belief about the nature of reality itself.[29] This basic belief constitutes the guiding principle at the heart of the educational process. If it commands the assent of teacher and taught, it will provide the common ground on which sound relationships can grow, and the disciplinary framework without which sound learning cannot take place.

CONSENSUS

Ideally, the guiding principle should be arrived at by a consensus, freely arrived at, between teacher and taught. In the world of compulsory, non-voluntary schooling this is clearly not so. The objects of the exercise are conscripts, and the teacher-pupil relationship is bedevilled from the outset. Enlightenment is, or perhaps is not, transmitted through a medium which, lacking the essential element of consensus, becomes an amalgam of linguistic, cultural, religious, philosophical, historical and other substitutes. The medium is not the message, but its transparency, or opacity, which rests on the degree of consensus, undoubtedly affects the result.

Although it might be argued in favour of non-voluntary systems that a kind of consensus – a *modus vivendi* – can be arrived at, based on the self-interest of the parties concerned, the truth is that in practice a code is imposed unilaterally. Herein originates the problem affecting all teachers – how to achieve the willing acceptance by their pupils of the moral imperatives they seek to impose.

According to the manner in which this problem is solved, the order and discipline, indispensable to teaching and learning, will be, or will not be achieved. Where there is no consensus the system will have an inbuilt requirement to indoctrinate, that is to compel the conscripts to accept the guiding principle without which 'education' cannot happen, and in that way obtain their conformity with the ethos of the community the educational system exists to serve. The moral enigma in education therefore has to do with the notion of indoctrination in the pejorative meaning of the word, so often imputed to religious educational systems but in some sense contained in all.

In systems which are unequivocally religious in character, as are the Roman Catholic, Islamic or Jewish systems of today, a guiding principle is arrived at, in principle, through acceptance by teacher and taught of the tenets of a religion. Morality and faith are seen to be inextricably intertwined, and the question whether morality can or should be taught independently of religious belief becomes irrelevant. In such systems the integration of religious faith and morality is their inspiration and driving force, and provided that their tenets are freely accepted by those taught the charge of indoctrination cannot be brought against them. The recognition of the right of parents to represent their children as long as they are in the status of pupil is therefore crucial to the working of systems of this sort. It is worth noting that fascist, national socialist or communist systems also brought the force of a quasi-religious belief to their educational systems, but dispensed with the notion of consensus or approval by parents.

Christianity was the source of the guiding principle of the education that nurtured European civilisation. Moral education was intimately linked with the religious stances of society as a whole. Education was grounded in a consensus which was the source of the teacher's moral authority over pupils, to whom the teacher stood *in loco parentis*. The present-day problems facing educators have to be examined in the light of this declining tradition.

THE SCOTTISH EXPERIENCE

The Scottish experience may illustrate the point. Both before and after the Protestant Reformation, the integration of moral education and religious belief was at the heart of the educational exercise, and the social order benefited because the schools took such pains to instil basic Christian morality. When the universities became the crucibles of the Scottish Enlightenment, practices in education founded on religious observances on which an earlier age had laid great emphasis were gradually abandoned. The linkage of moral and religious education was attenuated, and 'a system of schools originally intended to make the population fit citizens of a Godly Commonwealth, came instead to fit them for the role of pioneers in a successful materialist state'.[30] The link was further stretched when the Education Act of 1872 decreed that religious instruction could take place only at prescribed parts of the school day. Secular education, which was compulsory, and religious education, which was not, were to be treated as separate disciplines. This division brought about confusion in the understanding of the true nature of religious education, and indeed about the educational process itself. The national system ceased to be 'unequivocally religious', and the traditional underpinning of moral education by religious belief crumbled.[31]

> Since the Enlightenment ... our view of the world is inevitably modified ... old certainties and absolutes ... [have been] exchanged for a scientific approach to knowledge ... [we] regard moral choices as provisional, and religious affinities as more a

matter of taste and breeding than of conviction. The new pieties are agnosticism, pluralism and toleration … We have not only stopped believing in God, we have stopped believing in ourselves. The root cause of the malaise … [is] an absence of any shared understanding of the purpose of human existence. Common culture [is] almost impossible to sustain without religion.[32]

In Scotland in 1918 the absorption of the voluntary sector into the national system introduced a further complication. With the school leaving age standing at fourteen, the education authority could argue that since pupils were subject to parental control, compulsory attendance at school could be justified as long as parents gave their consent, and this recognition of the primacy of parental authority helped to make the system viable.

After 1945, the situation changed. The leaving age was raised to fifteen and then to sixteen, with additional requirements for the sixteen to eighteen age group. Relevance of parental authority weakened. Moral uncertainties infected the country and consequently the schools.

Since 1872 … a position [arose] which has contributed to the present malaise … On moral education, no education authority in Scotland makes any specific recommendations or requirements, and nor has any person been specially appointed to advise on or develop moral education.[33]

If there is to be a universally acceptable national educational system in our pluralist and post-Christian society, some other, ostensibly non-religious guiding principle has to be found on which it can be based, capable of being implemented without the kind of sanctions that are founded on faith in religious systems.

Awareness of this need was evident in the philosophy that underlay the introduction of guidance systems in Scottish secondary schools in the 1970s. It was suggested that pupils should work out for themselves, through group discussions and in other ways, a code of moral standards which they could accept and understand.[34] The hope was that by this approach their free acceptance of a code would be more readily achieved than by the imposition of moral imperatives from above. The suggestion was a remarkable departure from traditional Scottish educational practice, as well as a bypassing of centuries of Christian experience. It was also out of harmony with Judaic and Islamic tradition. Whereas no one would begin teaching engineering to a primitive society by asking them to re-invent the wheel, something comparable was being suggested in this matter of a code. Protagoras' doubtful dictum, that 'Man is the measure of all things', was being abandoned, and the child substituted for ancient wisdom. The policy had a further flaw, in that it had not sought the approval of the parents, or teachers who were to implement it.

It should be noted, in parenthesis, that one outcome of this policy was the endorsement of non-directive counselling, which is surely a contradiction in terms. Signposts or maps, which give guidance to the traveller, do not have to be followed, but they do need to point in the proper direction; counsellors likewise cannot compel obedience, but they should be prepared to point to the direction they themselves would follow and give reasons for their decisions. The best of all guides in difficult or unknown terrain is not a map or a signpost, but one who walks with the wayfarer. 'Everyman, I will go with thee, and be thy guide.'

The question to be faced by a non-religious or secular educational system is whether a new consensus can be reached on a guiding principle that is independent of religious beliefs and capable of sustaining a satisfactory code of behaviour. Current official wisdom appears to accept that it is possible.

It is possible to show moral concern and commitment without

necessarily basing this on a religious view of life. Philosophically, psychologically and sociologically a case can be made for the independence of morality from religion.[35]

The proposition is debatable. When Rousseau faced it, he had to take refuge in the concept of conscience, 'thou divine instinct … thou infallible judge of good and evil',[36] leaving open the problem of justifying the nature and reliability of conscience. A report to the General Assembly of the Church of Scotland in 1982, which concluded that people are capable of moral insight without making a religious confession of faith, and can use moral concepts independently of religious ones, nevertheless had to concede that in face of such fundamental questions as, Why be good, or, Why bother about moral issues, morality does require some ultimate justification, in terms of either religion or philosophy.[37] It was Gilson, a leading neo-Thomist philosopher of the twentieth century, who pointed out that failing a rational justification of morality, and granting that morality is inseparable from human life, for those who reject a religious basis for morality, there is nothing to do but take morality as a self-justifying fact.[38]

In the real world of the schoolroom, inhabited by real children, teachers have to grapple with this and similar questions. There is a vacuum that needs to be filled, with a philosophy providing a more acceptable base for the authority of the teacher over the pupil, than a simple *fiat* from above. Nor do the problems end there. Practising what is preached remains a difficulty no matter where the code originates. Even where pupils have worked out their own code of moral standards, it has often proved difficult to encourage them to apply these standards to their own actions.

Teachers have to be concerned, not only with filling the philosophical vacuum, but also with the problem of making moral education effective. In order to have any credibility in the eyes of their pupils, they themselves have to be committed to the guiding principle on which their ethical stance is based. Commitment to it, and to attitudes such as devotion to duty, strict fidelity or conscientiousness, which are necessary for the effective communication of that stance, is of the nature of religion, and it could therefore be said that moral education partakes of the nature of a religious exercise.

It is impossible to deny the link between religion and morality.... How one acts depends ultimately on what one believes – that is to say, on a creed – about the nature of humanity and of reality.[39]

RESPECT FOR PERSONS

No society has yet solved the problem of how to teach morality without religion.... Moral education without reference to religious belief would be an arid, de-personalised and ineffective exercise.[40]

Napoleon could not conceive of a popular education that did not have a religious basis. In his view there could be no state without morality, no morality without religion:

Without morality I do not see any real prosperity for empires, and without religion I do not know any true morality. The foundation of law is God; hence, no separation between politics and religion. In the matter of popular education, the State and the Church are the only effective powers.[41]

The most evident bridge between morality and religion is the idea of virtue. Moral philosophy must include this dimension whether we call it religion or not.[42]

We all approve of truthfulness, kindness and courage: we all disapprove of dishonesty, cruelty and cowardice. The human virtues at the domestic level are not really in dispute.[43]

What might qualify as a basis for a non-religious morality of the post-Christian, post-modern period is respect for persons, or the concept of the inviolability of human rights. While these concepts have something to recommend them, they require a philosophical justification with a foundation in reality if they are not to be accepted simply as self-justifying facts, and if they are to be given the commitment to them by teachers that is necessary for their effective transmission to succeeding generations. That justification rests on the conviction that human beings are of unique value, and it is because of the element of truth in that conviction that these concepts have viability. In effect, that conviction is supported by the religious belief that persons are made in the image of God. Without that belief, however, these propositions become fundamentally fragile, lacking a sense of transcendence of the natural order and unable to withstand the pressures of utilitarian materialism. In a world dominated by a purely materialist philosophy, respect for persons is not likely to triumph over self-interest, nor bring about the kind of commitment to it that is necessary if a civilisation is to live by it. Those who do not believe in God, have to find another justification for their attachment to the notion of respect for persons, which for them becomes a matter of faith.

MORALITY – A UNIVERSAL ELEMENT

Morality is something more than the consensus of a particular society. Some principles, such as the concept of justice, are found in all cultures and in all ages.[44] The passions aroused by infringements of codes of behaviour at many sporting encounters are evidence of the universality of the hunger for justice. Consider what happens when a deliberate foul is committed on the football field, a wrong line-call is made on the tennis court, a cricketer is given a doubtful leg-before decision, or a golfer is found to have adjusted the lie. In such cases the destructive character of the act comes primarily from its being a deliberate infringement of a consensus which has been freely accepted about how the game should be played. Hence professional fouls are more heinous than accidental infringements of the laws of the game, and can appear in certain circumstances as sins crying to heaven for vengeance. The reactions such transgressons arouse indicate that the hunger and thirst for justice is universal.

The Christian tradition recognises this universal element in human behaviour as a law of nature. If a guiding principle of morality is applicable to all people and at all times, there is clearly a need to ask, where does such a law come from? The Christian, Judaic and Islamic answer would attribute it to the action of God.

> Body and Soul are inseparable in the person; in the willing agent and in the deliberate act, they stand or fall together. Freedom and nature belong always together. Natural Law is universal, extends to all mankind. There is something in man that transcends cultures.... In the depths of his conscience man detects a law which he does not impose on himself, but which holds him to obedience.... Conscience does not formulate the law of which it is aware, but applies it in particular circumstances.[45]

MORAL EDUCATION IS FOUNDED ON FAITH

To recapitulate: any educational code will have to have regard for the intellectual and spiritual essence of teacher and taught. It will require to have a principle from which to start – a *point de départ* – which commands acceptance by pupil and teacher and the community at large. In practice this will acquire the force of a creed. Moral education has therefore to be founded on faith.

The respect accorded to the pupil by the teacher, and to the teacher by the pupil, will find justification in whatever belief is held by both about the nature of persons, just as the respect, or lack of it towards the subjects of study will also be founded on some basic belief about the nature of reality itself. A code founded on a Pythagorean view of harmony in nature will result in a different hierarchy of subjects than one based on Socratic principles or on a theory of evolution. A code which stresses the importance of individual effort will differ in essence from one emphasising the centrality of communal action, or from one that requires conformity with imposed lines of thinking.

Codes can give expression to different views of the potentiality of the pupils, as well as of the value of the subject-matter being presented. Commitment to a guiding principle about the nature of reality will provide the common ground on which sound relationships can grow. Such commitment, rooted in conscientiousness, is of the essence of religion. While no 'logical' demonstration of the connection between moral education and formal religion could likely be constructed, it is surely impossible to deny the link between them.

A GLOBAL ETHIC

As the Third Millenium advances, educational systems of the Anglophone world are having to provide for ever-greater numbers of students from a wide range of religious and linguistic backgrounds. At present their needs are being met in Catholic, Anglican, Jewish and non-denominational schools The question will arise whether separate schools for such immigrant communities should be instituted. Such a request has already been made by the Islamic community.

Whatever policy is officially adopted, a basic code will have to be found to underpin the educational system. The notion of a Global Ethic propounded by Hans Kung, essentially a consensus on binding values such as 'You shall not kill', 'You shall not steal', 'You shall not lie', 'you shall not abuse sexuality' has given a lead that could be helpful to an educational system faced with a plurality of religious traditions.[46]

4

Religious Education
The Teacher as Minister

What a piece of work is man! How noble in reason! How infinite in faculty! In form and moving how express and admirable! In action how like an angel! In apprehension how like a god.

Shakespeare, *Hamlet*

It is not true, as has been said, that today there are no gods and precious few heroes.[47] Examples abound of altruistic self-giving, as heroic in peace-time as much as in war. Lifeboat crews, helicopter pilots, nurses, doctors and firemen are a few examples. If self-sacrifice is taken as the indicator of an heroic life-style, nuns, priests, ministers of religion and teachers might qualify. And mothers. There are also many gods, most of them, unfortunately, strange, in defiance of the biblical command.[48]

What is true is that there is an intimate relationship between spirituality, self-sacrifice and education.

It is an innate propensity of humankind to ask why things are as they are. The thirst for truth is so deeply rooted that 'one may define the human being as the one who seeks the truth … People seek a final explanation, a supreme value, which refers to nothing beyond itself and puts an end to all questioning … Personal existence must be anchored to a truth recognised as final'.[49] One who devotes his or her life unremittingly to that search might well be described as heroic.

An education that fails to take account of this aspect of the human condition will be little more than a technical training, which could prove inhuman and destructive. Teachers must seek the truth about the nature of mankind and therefore of the whole of reality, and in so doing they enter, perforce, the field of religion. The answers they find will determine the kind of education they provide.[50]

For the Finnish composer Rautavaara, religion is 'a sense of and a taste for the eternal'.[51] This is not a definition of a structured faith. Rather it is a description of 'religiousness', a universal characteristic of humanity. In their concept expressed in the word *numen* the Romans recognised that characteristic. When Einstein considered the nature of religion, he did not attempt a definition, but asked instead what it is that characterises a religious person. He then gave his own answer – the religious person is one who is liberated from selfish desires, and preoccupied with thoughts, feelings and aspirations to which he clings because of their supra-personal value. What matters is the supra-personal content, and the strength of the conviction of its overpowering meaningfulness, regardless of whether any attempt is made to unite this with a Divine being or not.[52] In this view religion is a personal matter, demanding commitment on the part of the individual. It is not clear if Einstein distinguished between a philosophy and a religion.

In consideration of the same question the *Oxford Companion to Philosophy* describes religion as an aspect of experience which attempts to combine the scientific aim, of giving an account of the world as it is in itself, and the artistic aim, of giving a vision of the world adapted to human sensory faculties and emotional sensibilities.[53] In this view, religion reveals the world as informed by purpose, will and personality, and as expressing the intentions of a transcendent being. Religious insight is held to be necessary to arrive at the truth about things, and to reach the fullness of development that is an aim of education.

These views, which attempt to discuss the nature of religion without reference to any revelation, are widely supported:

[Poetics, music and art] enact … a root-impulse of the human spirit to explore possibilities of meaning and … truth that lie outside empirical seizure or proof.[54]

The development of science and technology … does not free humanity from the obligation to ask the ultimate religious questions.[55]

Faith in God is … the only guarantee of a genuine understanding and respect for human dignity.… Those who have abandoned belief in God … have a fundamentally different understanding of what constitutes human nature and the proper ordering of society.[56]

Neither religion nor morality has its full meaning unless they penetrate each other.[57]

There is no unconditionally binding ethic without a religious base.[58]

Religion is the art of giving without strings attached.[59]

In the far reaches of the human heart there is a seed of desire and nostalgia for God.[60]

Religious attitudes are so widespread as to constitute a necessary element in human life, and therefore have to be addressed in a complete educational programme.

RELIGION IN EDUCATION

The ethos, or cultural tone of a community is a function of its value system, of its fundamental beliefs, and of the way in which practical expression is given to those beliefs.

An educational system reflects the religious attitudes of the community it serves. Where the people are of one mind in faith and culture, religion and morality are inextricably intertwined, and together provide an element that binds society together. Religious education aims towards nurturing a shared belief about the nature of reality, giving instruction in the good life as it is understood, explaining its significance in the history of the community, and giving guidance on how its values might be sustained. If the pupil is a willing disciple of the faith of the community, his or her personal integrity and freedom will not be contravened by the requirement to learn about that faith. 'The spiritual growth of pupils should not be looked at in an individualistic way ... pupils come to school not as isolated individuals, but as members of a social, political and religious community.' The pupil's search after truth in any subject is capable of including a religious dimension.[61]

Christianity is an historic religion, rooted in Judaism, sharing with it a concept of morality enshrined in the two great commandments of love. In Christian revelation human beings are seen to be imperfect but redeemed, and of infinite value. Christian education has to take account of this imperfection, while recognising the implications of redemption. An essential element in this recognition is an understanding of the interdependence of love and sacrifice.

Christian education, which aims to bring faith, culture and life into harmony, has to be directed towards the moral and spiritual as well as the intellectual faculties. It is therefore distinguished from systems in which religion is regarded as an academic subject like any other. Because of its integration of faith and morals, Christian teachers accept a responsibility for the moral and spiritual welfare of their pupils that extends beyond the satisfying of intellectual and vocational needs. They have to be witnesses to the faith they profess. 'The teacher's commitment to a view of reality is explicitly, in design and intent, the primary resource out of which religious education flows, and by means of which it is nourished and developed.'[62] That commitment arises from faith in the doctrine being taught. So-called non-religious systems are also based on faith – only the gods are different.

> The Christian religion was influential in the formation and development of Scottish nationhood and national identity from the start ... from the mediaeval period through centuries of Scottish Reformation and Enlightenment down to the industrial epoch of Victorian and Edwardian Scotland.[63]

Scottish education was an expression of the nation's Christian heritage and its commitment to that tradition. Now, those who strive to uphold that tradition are in danger of being overwhelmed. Two strands persist, represented by the denominational and non-denominational sectors. Both are struggling in the secular atmosphere of the society they serve. Both are expected to give to education a moral dimension, recognised as necessary both by the community at large and by the funding authority. The non-denominational sector has to find a quasi-religious or philosophical justification for the moral education it provides, while the denominational sector has to present, within the limits of a structure which marginalises the religious education on which its moral dimension is based, an integrated Christian view of the human condition that takes account of modern scientific thinking,

In the Catholic sector, where the Christian tradition survives most strongly, a situation has developed in which religious education becomes as it were an extra bolted on to the curriculum, in schools which in some ways are almost indistinguishable from their non-denominational counterparts. In these circumstances it is difficult to give full expression to the Christian ethos. 'Young people should find revelation in all of their lives – in their love and pain, their experience of community – as well as in the formal teaching of Christian doctrine.'[64] However, neither schools nor teachers are autonomous, and cannot be more powerful witnesses to the Christian message than the community of which they are a part.

MORALITY AND RELIGION IN EDUCATION

The integration of the spiritual dimension into the curriculum is a matter of supreme importance, as well as of great delicacy. As has been argued above, all education is moral education, and moral education, to be effective, requires the support of a code, or belief, that has the force of a religious faith. There is therefore a temptation in any educational system to introduce some supportive belief on the basis of which acceptance of the desired ethical system can be achieved – or, more likely – enforced. Thus educators, following the practice of others who have to protect a position of authority, sometimes fall victim to the temptation to seize the high moral ground with a view to gaining the obedience of the subjects. Typically this is done by imposing some arbitrary requirement, as for example by asserting that it is unseemly, or even immoral, to avoid wearing a school uniform.

Some would contend that such an attitude – that is, the enforcement of an ethical system without consensus – can be justified by the positive academic attainment that may result, or by the contribution that schools make to civil harmony if the necessary discipline is gained. It is an attitude which implies that some supportive belief may be introduced to justify the imposition of discipline, irrespective of whether or not that belief is true. The end, in short, justifies the means. If adopted in the matter of religious education, however, the approach is fatally flawed. The justification for the religious dimension of an educational system must lie in the fact that through it there is presented an aspect of the truth about the human condition that is necessary for the full development of the pupil and is delivered in no other way.

A distinctive aspect of the present – first decade twenty-first century – Scottish system is its dual approach to the religious dimension in education.

In the latter half of the twentieth century, the situation of religious education in the non-denominational sector was fundamentally different from that of the denominational sector.

In the decades that followed World War II the deep-seated spiritual malaise of society at large penetrated the whole of the national educational community. A loss of moral certainty in the adult population, experienced nationwide, resulted in the erosion of parental authority and confusion in the minds of the young, and led to a crisis in moral and religious education, which elicited responses from both civil and ecclesiastical authorities. Following the Millar Report on Moral and Religious Education in 1972, a structure of personal, vocational and curricular guidance was introduced into secondary schools; a Teaching Qualification in Religious Education for Secondary Education was introduced in 1974, and Specialist Teachers of Religious Education began to be trained to meet the consequent curricular demands. This led in turn to the development of Religious Studies as an examinable subject. Section 66 (2) of the Education (Scotland) Act 1980, which forbade inspection of Religious Instruction by H. M. Inspectorate, was repealed by the Education (Scotland) Act 1981, and in 1983 government inspection of Religious Education began.

These changes marked a paradigm shift in the approach to Religious Education, which was no longer being seen as a responsibility of every teacher. They were resisted to some extent, but the marginalisation of Religious Education that followed, particularly at the secondary level, combined with the alienation of the rising generations from the mainstream churches tended to stultify the aims of Christian educators. Traditional concepts of the integrating aspect of religious education, and of the nature of knowledge, were radically affected. In the ancient tradition memory, understanding and will were seen as powers of the soul, and therefore the cultivation of these powers, even when concerned with secular matters, shared in the transcendence of religious education.

> Knowledge is not merely verbal, but a kind of divine science. It is that light which is kindled in the soul … and which makes manifest all created things and teaches man to know both himself and all that he may be able to understand through his reason.[65]

> The image of the 'Universal Man' is disappearing more and more. Nevertheless it remains each man's duty to preserve a view of the whole human person, a view in which the values of intellect, will, conscience and fraternity are pre-eminent.[66]

In the schools of the denominational sector – at present almost exclusively Roman Catholic – the place and aim of Religious Education remained fairly clear: it is to bear witness to and inform pupils, in ways suited to age and ability, of the doctrines of their faith community, and to clarify the implications of that faith for the way of life that is being presented to them for their acceptance. In such a system, there is an obligation on all its proponents to uphold its fundamental teaching and so keep faith with the parents who have committed the upbringing of their children to it. Religious attitudes must, of necessity, inform the whole curriculum, and it is therefore reasonable to hold that in such a system all education is religious education.

It does have some in-built difficulties. Institutions which uphold the primacy of conscience, and maintain that the laws of charity are the essence of their teaching, must act fittingly within these parameters. Again, the content of academic teaching should not be self-contradictory: it should not, for example, teach the over-arching power of God as creator and supporter of the universe in one area of the curriculum, and in another imply that the universe proceeds in a purely materialistic and mechanical way; or appear to teach that the history of mankind can be understood without reference to the God it believes in.

Denominational schools are subject to the regulations about guidance and religious education that are outlined above. They are required by law to be open to all, whether believers or not, and in consequence are becoming, in greater or less degree, reflections of the multicultural and multi-faith society that the community has become. This poses problems for religious education and the ethos of the schools, in addition to those arising from the difficulties inherent in the work of religious education itself.

The educational system as a whole was readjusting to conformity with the ethos of the wider community, in an attempt to fill the vacuum left by the decline in church membership. It now has to confront the problem of integrating the element of spiritual awareness with its moral consensus in a way that will command the agreement of parents and pupils as well as the commitment of the teachers who have to uphold it.

RELIGIOUS EDUCATION AND RELIGIOUS STUDIES

At the end of the second millenium of the Christian era, formal dependence on religion as the basis for education was so eroded that a fresh reappraisal of the place of Christianity, or indeed of religion as such, in the educational system was required. A start was made by the introduction into the curriculum of the subject of Religious Studies, an academic subject concerned with learning about different religious traditions, without a requirement, by teacher or pupil, of commitment to any one of them.

In a multicultural society the case for its introduction is

strong. For an understanding of our own changing community, as well as of the wider world, some knowledge of the great religions of the world is necessary. However, Religious Studies cannot be a substitute for Religious Education. Because a religion is more than a philosophy, Religious Education has to be more than the imparting of knowledge and more than the recounting of history or the rational analysis of intellectual positions. Such exercises are more germane to Religious Studies than to Religious Education. Religious Studies deals with a branch of general knowledge that should be part, some might argue the most important part, of the History, Geography or Modern Studies curriculum, preferably of all three.[67]

The function of the Christian teacher is not merely to direct the study of some objective material, but to bear witness to a set of propositions about the past, the present and the future which are held to be true. This is the justification for religious education in any faith-based educational system, and was formerly true of the Scottish tradition.

All education, it could be argued, is religious education – or at least is about religiousness.

RELIGIOUS EDUCATION AND SCIENCE

> Recent studies and findings of science, history and philosophy raise new questions which influence life and demand new theological investigations … Appropriate use must be made … of the findings of the secular sciences, especially of psychology and sociology. Let the Church also acknowledge new forms of art adapted to our age.[68]

The current cultural climate in which Christian educators live is dominated by scientific materialism. Today, perhaps only temporarily, physics has ousted metaphysics from its position of philosophical dominance – although some physicists now seem to be bringing it back. Although there can be no fundamental contradiction between scientific and religious truth, it is the case that the mindset demanded by a modern scentific outlook is difficult to reconcile with one demanding an intuitive recognition of the transcendental aspect of reality.

Historically, religious truth has been tied to statements about the nature of the cosmos that are essentially of a scientific rather than a religious character. In the modern era some part of the loss of confidence in the truth of Christianity is the result of scientific advance. To meet the needs of the rising generations Christian educators need both knowledge of the historical experience of the Christian community, and understanding of the interaction of philosophy, theology, metaphysics and scientific knowledge in the unfolding of insight into the message of the Gospel. These requirements are approached in the following chapters.

5

The Mysterious Universe
The Teacher as Cosmologist

Except for children (who don't know enough not to ask the important questions) few of us spend much time wondering whether … there are ultimate limits to what humans can know.

Stephen Hawking, *A Brief History of Time*

Let no one ever, ever doubt what no one can be sure about.

Hilaire Belloc

In his study of the influence of scientific advance on western culture during the last three centuries, Whitehead wrote:

Faith in reason is the trust that the ultimate nature of things lie together in a harmony which excludes mere arbitrariness. It is the faith that at the base of things we shall not find mere arbitrary mystery. The faith in the order of nature which has made possible the growth of science is a particular example of a deeper faith … [which] cannot be justified by any inductive generalisation. It springs from direct inspection of the nature of things as disclosed in our own immediate experience.… To experience this faith is to know that in being ourselves we are more than ourselves: to know that our experience, dim and fragmentary as it is, yet sounds the utmost depths of reality; to know that detached details … demand that they should find themselves in a system of things; to know that this system includes the harmony of logical rationality, and the harmony of aesthetic achievement; to know that, while the harmony of logic lies upon the universe as an iron necessity, the aesthetic harmony stands before it as a living ideal moulding the general flux in its broken progress towards finer, subtler issues.[69]

Advances in knowledge and technology during the past two hundred years have rendered ever more acute the problems of harmonising the mental sets demanded by the apparently conflicting truths of religion and science.

While the volume and diversity of the elements which make up culture increase, at the same time the capacity of individual men to perceive them and to blend them organically decreases, so that the image of the universal man becomes ever more faint.... Recent studies and findings of science, history and philosophy raise new questions which influence life and demand new theological investigations.... Appropriate use must be made ... of the findings of the secular sciences, especially of psychology and sociology. Let the Church also acknowledge the new forms of art adapted to our age.[70]

Confidence in the truths of the Christian faith has been undermined by scientific advance. For those who believe that the unity of truth is a fundamental premise of human reasoning and that therefore the truth conferred by revelation is to be understood in the light of reason, the need to bring into harmony and integrate the truths of science and religion has become a central, demanding issue.[71]

In the educational field the problems are raised most acutely by pupils at the adolescent stage, and their resolution left more and more to teachers. As a result they are having to fulfil a philosophical-theological role for which they have neither the authority nor preparation. If they fail to rise to the challenge, they lose face; if they attempt to shoulder the burden, they act *ultra vires*.

The overarching educational aim of the Protestant Reformers of 1560 was 'the godly upbringing of youth', a notion which had its origin in Saint Augustine's *City of God*, was taken up by Calvin and carried to Scotland from Geneva. The educational system which resulted functioned on a theocentric basis as long as it was under the under the control of the Kirk. Over time this foundation in religion was gradually eroded, more particularly when the secular ideas of the Enlightenment, which saw the present as the only world worth striving for, began to percolate the national culture. An educational ethos developed in which truth and knowledge were sought as the route to mastery of nature, to be rewarded by prosperity in this world as well as eternal happiness in the next.

In this scenario the idea with the greatest impact on the theory and practice of education was the notion, associated especially with Rousseau, of the natural goodness of mankind. The implications of this abandonment of the age-old acceptance that children can be spoiled if they lack firm direction are still being worked out today. Denying, as it does, the doctrine that human nature is in some fundamental sense flawed, it takes as a corollary the view that mankind can attain its own greatest good unaided, by its own exertions and through the operation of natural reason. With the acceptance of this philosophical stance, an anthropocentric view of the universe had triumphed. Educators abandoned the teaching of Saint Augustine on which the system had been founded, and adopted instead the position of Pelagius his redoubtable opponent.[72]

In the latter part of the nineteenth century the religious basis of education was further eroded by a scientific and philosophical revolution that shook the foundations of Christian belief. Following the publication of *On the Origin of Species* in 1859, powerful voices, T.H. Huxley's and Matthew Arnold's among them, called for changes in the school curriculum even at the elementary stage. In 1861 the power of the Church of Scotland to approve or examine teachers was taken from the Presbytery and given to the universities. When the State finally took command of the national educational system in 1872 it became an important part of national policy to foster the study of the new science.[73] Religious and secular education were seen as separate activities, with religion pushed to the margin, except in the Catholic and Episcopalian sectors which remained outside state control.

The twentieth century was only a few years old when Max Planck introduced the concept of quantum mechanics, and hard on its heels came Einstein's theory of Relativity. Decades later these near-mystical ideas were just beginning to percolate the national culture and the vastly expanded schools system. When *The Mysterious Universe*[74] appeared in 1930, the author, Sir James Jeans, wrote

> There is a widespread conviction that the new teachings of astronomy and physical science are destined to produce an immense change on our outlook on the universe as a whole, and on our views as to the significance of human life. The question at issue is ultimately one for philosophical discussion, but … science ought first be asked to tell all she can as to ascertained facts and provisional hypotheses. Then, and then only, may discussion legitimately pass into the realms of philosophy.

Jeans, however, had already entered the philosophical realm. What did he mean by the word 'mysterious'? Was he implying, like traditionalists, that the universe is so far beyond our ken that it can never be completely understood? Or, that it was mysterious only in the limited sense that it could be fully grasped by the human mind, when all necessary facts and clues became available? In 1930 he appeared to lean towards the second view. Now, a psalmist's lifetime later, it is by no means certain that all physicists would agree with him. At least one, John D. Barrow, questions whether there may be limits to human discovery, a frontier beyond which lies the unknowable, the unthinkable.[75] His is a view which is in accord with the traditional Christian meaning of mystery, signifying truth which is beyond or above reason.

This issue is only one of many that modern scientific thought poses for the educator. If those who uphold the Christian tradition hope to counter effectively the spirituality of the present age, they too must be prepared to give an account of their worldview in language that speaks to the scientifically-minded and freedom-conscious people of this time. Perhaps the time is right for seeking answers to questions raised by Pope John Paul II in an address to scientists at a Colloquy at Castel Gondolpho in 1987:

> Is Christianity ready to form a deeper collaboration with science, a more powerful interchange in which the integrity of both is maintained and the advance of each fostered? Is the scientific community ready to work more closely with other communities, including the religious community, making no decisions about religion but working with the Church to build a culture that is more in keeping with human dignity?

He noted a 'definite though still fragile and provisional movement towards a new and more nuanced interchange between religion and science', and saw

> an unprecedented opportunity for a common relationship in which each discipline retains its integrity and yet is radically open to the discoveries and insights of the other ... science can purify religion from error and superstition; religion can purify science from idolatry and false absolutes ... our knowledge of each other can lead us to be more authentically ourselves.... The human community which we both serve has a right to demand such interaction from us.[76]

Such interaction is not unprecedented. In the past, some elements of religious truth were tied to descriptions of the cosmos that were scientific rather than religious in character, and in consequence, in the development of western

Christian culture, the understanding of the religious truth contained in the message of revelation has had to be restated in the light of scientific advance.

An example of such revision can be seen in how the concept of space presented in Genesis was altered by the advent of Newtonian physics. The biblical description of the creation of the world posits in the beginning of time a 'vault' that separated the waters above from the waters below. This could be interpreted as a first approximation to a theory of space, conceived of as an inner space (the vault) within which the work of creation took place, and an outer space, occupied by 'the waters', about which nothing further is said or known (this concept is examined more fully in Appendix 3).

This spatial framework was admirably suited to accommodate a Ptolemaic and theocentric vision of the cosmos, which dominated Christendom throughout the first millenium. During the second, the Christian concept of reality developed for the most part in the aftermath of shocks imparted by major scientific discoveries or theories, expounded in turn by Buridan, Copernicus, Descartes, Darwin, Freud, Planck, Einstein and Heisenberg, and by the discoverers of DNA. When, after Copernicus, the system of classical physics began to be formed, the description of the cosmos required a changed view of space, in which the space within the vault was seen to be infinite, i.e. of unknown extent, but had nothing to say of what might lie beyond. In this classical, Newtonian view, space was infinite, homogeneous and featureless; mere emptiness like the vacuum of the ancient atomists.[77] The basic religious message of a contingent universe, that is of a universe that did not exist of itself, but was created by God and supported by Him, was left unchanged.

Newton was able to describe and quantify the force of gravity, but could give no explanation of how it could act at a distance, and fell back on a mediaeval description of it as an occult force. His thinking made no provision for the interaction of spiritual with corporeal being. He considered himself primarily a theologian, and was aware of the need to fuse science and theology at least in his own mind. His theology was not simply a handmaiden to his science. He was greatly interested in Biblical chronology, seen as the working out of God's Plan, and saw science as the unfolding of another Divine Plan. In his view God had two roles – as Creator and as sustainer of the universe, a concept that seems to have been drawn from the Thomistic view of the contingent nature of the cosmos. He asked if the world came about by chance, or by choice by some intelligent agent. He noted design in many instances, and held that God has to act at all times to keep gravity going. For Newton, God is a ruler having constant dominion, who sustains duration and space. In Him are all things contained and moved. In this view, science does not threaten religion, if science is right. Newton's true science does not threaten. False religious beliefs lead to false science, true science leads to true God.[78]

Newtonian classical mechanics envisaged the physical world as made up of matter and radiation, the matter consisting of atoms and the radiation of wave motion. Waves, however, cannot undulate in nothingness, and so the idea of something called ether had to be postulated to fill the vacuum of space and provide the medium necessary for wave motion to take place.

The concept of ether was altogether too ethereal to last, and had soon to be abandoned. About the beginning of the twentieth century Planck introduced a new concept, which was a complete break with the classical tradition. He supposed that radiation was carried through the ether, not in a continuous stream as sound waves are through air or water, but in discrete packets, called quanta, and therefore had a kind of atomic structure analogous to that which appeared to be so well established in the case of matter. Of special philosophical interest was the discovery that the amount of energy in a quantum of radiation bore a constant relation to its frequency. Known as Planck's Constant, this was found to be a universal constant of nature.

The theory succeeded because it accounted for, and in some cases predicted, observable phenomena which defied explanation on Newtonian principles. However, when Einstein's enunciation in 1905 of the Theory of Relativity led to inferences incompatible with the existence of any kind of ether, the classical understanding of gravitation was superseded by Einstein's, and this revolutionary change was followed by others. Bohr's discoveries, published in 1913, showed that there are events in the physical world that cannot be represented within the Newtonian framework of space and time. The age of classical physics which extended from the publication of Newton's *Principia* in 1687 to the acceptance of General Relativity and Quantum-Mechanics, came to an end, and with it a philosophical view of the cosmos that had held sway for about 250 years.[79]

These and other advances in science and astronomy leave unanswered the fundamental question of the nature and extent of space. In effect, human understanding of the vault within which creation takes place has been expanded to ever wider limits; but what lies beyond these limits remains unknown, some would say unknowable. Since the velocity of light is finite, a part of the universe existing at an infinite distance – if there is any such, and if that is an intelligible concept and not simply a collection of words – can never be known in the physical sense. The description of space as infinite is logically an assertion that space is beyond our comprehension.

The Star-gazer[80]

Forty-two years ago (to me if to no one else
The number is of some interest) it was a brilliant starry night
And the westward train was empty and had no corridors
So darting from side to side I could catch the unwonted sight
Of those almost intolerably bright
Holes, punched in the sky, which excited me partly because
Of their Latin names and partly because I had read in the
  textbooks
How very far off they were, it seemed their light
Had left them (some at least) long years before I was.

And this remembering now I mark that what
Light was leaving some of them at least then,
Forty-two years ago, will never arrive
In time for me to catch it, which light when
It does get here may find that there is not
Anyone left alive
To run from side to side in a late night train
Admiring it and adding noughts in vain.

The scientific revolutions of the twentieth century demand a further review of the relationship between religious and scientific truth, and an examination of their possible convergence and harmonisation.

THE UNCERTAINTY PRINCIPLE AND CAUSALITY

In the wonderful world of quantum physics events occur which cannot be exactly predicted. This is because quanta of radiation sometimes behave as solid particles, and sometimes as wave pulses. This mysterious phenomenon gave rise to Heisenberg's Uncertainty Principle, which states that if the position of a sub-atomic particle is known exactly then its momentum is completely uncertain. There is therefore an element of unpredictability about the behaviour of the particle, and so it has to be accepted that the causes involved in its movement are in some degree unknown, perhaps unknowable.

Because of these discoveries it has been claimed that the classical principle of cause and effect does not operate at that sub-atomic level of reality. It seems that yet again the traditional Christian view of the cosmos, which holds that the causal principle operates universally, has to suffer another readjustment in the light of scientific advance.

It is however not valid to conclude that occurrences which cannot be predicted do not have prior causes. All that can be fairly said is that the causes are unknown. Heisenberg himself resurrected the Aristotelian and Thomistic idea of intrinsic 'potentiality' to account for the element of unpredictability in some physical systems.

Science proceeds by observation and measurement, and by the construction of hypotheses which are tested by repeated experiment. Such testing assumes that the causes of the phenomena being observed operate in the same way on every occasion: that is, it assumes an underlying constancy in the principle of cause and effect. It is on this assumption that new discoveries are tested. If the results obtained are not as predicted, it is never the cause-effect principle that is discarded. This is a very common-sensible approach, accepted as axiomatic in the Christian tradition, but is nevertheless an assumption, a scientific article of faith.

Implicit also in the scientific method is a second assumption, that the cause-effect relationship as conceived in the mind of the observer corresponds to an objectively similar effect in the phenomena being observed. This fails to take account of the possibility that the cause-effect relationship might be something required by the observer's mode of thinking rather than being founded in the nature of the reality being observed. To be valid, it has to assume a constancy in the relationship of the observer to objective reality. To make this assumption again is eminently common-sensible, but it is nevertheless an article of scientific faith, also shared with the traditional Christian view.

CHAOS THEORY

If the unpredictability of certain phenomena were the result of a breakdown of the principle of cause and effect, then indeed the universe could be truly described as chaotic. Once upon a time such a catastrophe might have been attributed to some powerful and malevolent operator lurking in the depths of the mysterious electronic fields, with the power at will to alter the relationship of observer to reality. With such an evil demon in command, the cosmos would have been truly in chaos.[81]

For Plato, who discussed the notion, chaos was a disorderly primordial mass out of which was fashioned the ordered universe that he knew. Out of that chaos came order, but only through the action of a demiurge. To bring order into chaos, Plato had to presume the existence of an external agent, who, since the action was carried out on pre-existing chaotic matter, was not an omnipotent creator as in the Christian-Judaic tradition. The demiurge worked on something already existing, whereas the action of the biblical deity not only brought about an ordered universe, but called it into existence from nothing.

Chaos in the sense of total disorder is essentially undescribable. If the order that emerged from Plato's primordial chaos had come about without any outside interference, then there must have been a pre-existing potentiality of order within the mass, and therefore no total disorder. Total disorder implies the absence not only of order, but of everything that goes to make for order. Utter chaos has to include the notion of there not being even the potentiality of order within the chaotic system itself.

Some disorganised systems, so it is said, can spontaneously acquire organisation, just as a shapeless liquid mass can, upon cooling, solidify into an exquisite crystal.[82] In this case an apparently disorganised mass – disorganised only in the sense that the observer can see no order in it - acquires an observable order through the operation of physical and chemical laws of a universal character. The apparently disorganised mass is in a state of potential order, in that the physical laws that will make order visible are already implanted in the system.

Similarly, the term chaos has been used to denote the jumble of rocks at the foot of a scree slope, or the debris left by a retreating glacier. In these examples also the disorder is apparent, not real. The boulders at the foot of a scree slope or the debris left by a retreating glacier have been sorted out by natural forces, and their disposition is the result of the orderly operation of pre-existing physical laws. The disorder is in the mind of the beholder. For order to emerge out of 'chaos' the principle of cause and effect has to operate.

The fact that weather phenomena are not completely predictable does not mean that they are not subject to the laws of physics. Causal connections do exist within weather phenomena, and scientists construct models to explain them on that basis. The causes of the apparently disorderly occurrences of the *El Niño* phenomenon are being sought so that future occurrences can be predicted.

Lorenz, a meteorologist, examined the theory of apparently random behaviour in a deterministic system, such as the global weather system. His memorable example is of the 'butterfly effect', in which he suggested that the flap of a butterfly's wing in certain atmospheric circumstances could make the difference between a hurricane occurring or not occurring in some distant part of the world. The minute quantity of energy imparted by the flapping wings to a potentially unstable atmosphere at the extreme point of balance could, in theory, suffice to trigger a causal chain of events that with a kind of domino effect could lead, via a series of equally precariously balanced systems, to the release of enough energy to cause a hurricane. Clearly the final outcome, the consequence of an event that could not be observed, is unpredictable, but not uncaused.

Chaos theory suggests that apparently chaotic weather is a result, not of a lack of laws within a system, but of its being sensitive to minute and unobservable events affecting the initial conditions. Lorenz uses the notion to refer to processes whose variations are not random but look random, that appear to proceed according to chance even though the behaviour is in fact determined by precise laws. Jeans had already examined this process when he suggested that there is in the working of the universe, a certain amount of 'play',[83] such as happens in any old machine through wear and tear. He claimed that the fact that this 'play' pervades the whole universe destroys the case for strict causation, since this is a characteristic of perfectly fitting machinery. The conclusion is not valid. All that can be said is that the causes are not perceived, not understood, and perhaps not able to be perceived.

In the light of the amazing discoveries in the mysterious world of sub-atomic particles, the notion that there might be a demiurge, malevolent or not, at work now seems not quite so ridiculous as it once did. Are quarks angels or demons? How many quarks can dance on the point of a pin? In the Christian philosophical tradition these problems have been met and solved – a benevolent and all-powerful operator sustains the existence of everything, including quarks, and the objectivity, universality and constancy of the cause-effect principle.

CREATION – AN ACCIDENT?

Having disposed of the principle of cause and effect, Jeans went on to draw a further philosophical conclusion. 'Although we cannot speak with any certainty, it seems likely that humanity came into existence [as] the result of what may be properly be described as an accident.'[84] A dictionary definition of an accident is an unforeseen event, or one without an apparent cause. Jeans assumes that the origin of life was an event without a cause.

The traditional Christian view asserts that the existence of the cosmos requires the prior existence of an effective cause. If physicists accept that the cause-effect relationship is universally operative, then the philosophical case for an uncaused-cause, God, as the originator of the universe is difficult for them to combat. At least one concedes the point.

> We really have two choices when it comes to the origin of the universe. One is to say it was a supernatural event, and leave it at that. The other is to find some way of treating it as a natural event ... there will then be possibly an infinite number of other universes that can originate in the same manner. We're making huge assumptions about the nature of reality in postulating these other universes.[85]

Both Jeans and Hawking, examining the notion of accidental occurrences, refer to an idea, first propounded by T. H. Huxley, that if a number of monkeys were set to strum on typewriters for millions of years, they would be bound in time to write all the books in the British Museum. 'If we looked through all the millions of pages the monkeys had turned off in untold millions of years, we might be sure of finding a Shakespeare sonnet somewhere amongst them.'[86]

It is difficult to believe that any of these distinguished men saw this as a useful illustration of anything. It suggests that if an infinite number of monkeys worked on an infinite number of typewriters for an infinite period of time, they would produce every possible combination of all possible words made up of all the letters of the English alphabet, and ultimately every possible sequence of all these possible words. Within this totality would appear the whole of English literature. Setting aside for the moment the question whether the word 'infinite' has meaning in the real world, for this scenario to have even theoretical validity the monkeys themselves would have to have an infinite capacity for varying their actions, which is to say that they would not be monkeys. To produce every possible combination, of letters, words and sequences of words, some kind of ordered approach would have to be involved, and so, if a sonnet did emerge, it would not be an accidental occurrence.[87]

Modern theories about the origin of the universe have nothing to say about anything before the 'Big Bang', the singular event that marked the beginning of time. According to Hawking, 'if, as is the case, we know only what has happened since the 'Big Bang', we could not determine what happened beforehand ... events before can have no consequences ... time had a beginning at the big bang.'[88] Just as the work of creation took place within a space called 'the vault', and nothing is known outside it, so – in this view – creation took place in time, which also has a beginning before which nothing is known. Jeans came to the same conclusion. Arguing from the science of thermodynamics, and the concept of entropy which frowns upon the possibility of perpetual motion, he concluded that since entropy in the universe as a whole is still increasing, and so must have had a beginning; there must have been what we may describe as a 'creation' at a time not infinitely remote. 'If the universe is a universe of thought, then its creation must have been an act of thought ... modern scientific theory compels us to think of the creator as working outside time and space.' This accords with the conjecture of Augustine – *Non in tempore, sed cum tempore, finxit Deus mundum* (Not in time, but with time, did God make the world) – in which he is echoing Plato's conclusion, 'Time and the heavens came into being at the same instant.'

To the physical scientist the universe begins to look

more like a great thought than like a great machine. Mind no longer appears as an accidental intruder into the realm of matter.

We can most simply interpret consciousness as something residing entirely outside the continuum of space and time.[89]

If the work of creation is seen as an evolutionary process, then the existence of matter is the necessary precondition for the appearance, on earth, of spirit … the matrix of spirit … in which life emerges and is supported, not the active principle from which it takes its rise.[90]

THE ANTHROPIC PRINCIPLE

The laws of science, as we know them at present, contain many fundamental numbers, like the size of the electric charge on an electron.... The remarkable fact is that the values of these numbers seem to have been finely adjusted to make possible the development of life.... It seems clear that there are relatively few ranges of values for the numbers that would allow for the development of any form of intelligent life.[91]

Put simply, it appears that the universe had to be fine-tuned to allow for the development of life.

Whatever conclusions may be drawn from the findings of the modern physicists, one fact that seems to have certainty is that there are certain constants in place, existing since the Big Bang, without which intelligent life could not have come about. Planck's Constant is one example. These give whatever order there is to the material universe, and their existence may be evidence of the existence of an omnipotent being. The argument is a revised version of the age-old argument for the existence of God from the presence of order in the universe.

An approach, which assumes that there is a correspondence between human intelligence and the nature of things that will enable mankind of its own efforts to attain the fullness of truth, must allow at least the possibility that the scientific search may be approaching its ultimate end as it were asymptotically, always drawing closer to but never reaching the ultimate end, except at an infinitely distant point which is never reached in this life.

A NEW AGE

Through the two millenia of the Christian Era the religious truth enshrined in the biblical narrative, that the universe began as an act of will on the part of a Creator, has survived the changes in the concepts of the cosmos that resulted from each scientific advance. After the detonation of the atomic bomb in 1945 a new age dawned, Advances in fields other than theoretical physics raised issues that demand a rigorous disentanglement of religious and scientific truth. A revolution in genetics has spawned a new form of determinism impacting on the traditional view of the creation of the human species, and developments in other areas, such as neurology or psychology, have gone ahead without specific integration into the findings of physics.

Just as the task of mediaeval philosophy had been to remove the ground for conflict between philosophy and religion, so that of the philosopher in the present age is to reconcile religious and scientific truth. Both are founded on faith. The Christian-Judaic search is founded on an historic revelation, accepted by faith on a basis that is seen to be not unreasonable, and tested over time by human experience. 'The great moral insights of humanity were just as reasonable and true as the experimental findings of science and technology, indeed truer.'[92] The scientific procedure is also based on faith. It assumes the existence of order in the universe, and all scientific endeavour is directed towards understanding it. No one understands how consciousness comes about. All we can say is that it appears to have something to do with the complexity of the brain, probably one of the most complex structures to be found anywhere in the universe. It might be that the chances of life forms as advanced as ours emerging (elsewhere) are exceedingly remote. Indeed it might have happened only once in the history of the universe.

Although there is an acceptance by many scientists that the universe is built to be peculiarly hospitable to the kind of creatures we are, which may or may not be evidence of a designer, familiarity with transcendental reality is fading, with a consequent dire misunderstanding of the human condition and of the true nature and destiny of mankind. For the Christian educator, the need is to provide an integrated view of the cosmos, that will do justice to the truths and insights of both science and religion. It is a problem which tends to be left at the door of the practising teacher, who can hardly be blamed for thinking that finding the solutions lies beyond the call of duty.

6

Unity in Education and the Teacher

Ideally, the educational experience of an individual should lead to his harmonious and integrated development, and result in a person in command of himself and at peace with the universe.

E. Gilson, *The Unity of Philosophical Experience*

SOME SEMANTICS

What is to be understood by the expression Unity in Educational Experience?

Educational experience is something that can happen to an individual at any time of life, in any place and at any time, in or out of school. Living, breathing, eating, establishing relationships, singing, dancing, playing, being happy, being miserable, winning, losing, sleeping, waking, praying, loving, hating and so much else are involved. It is certainly not restricted to what happens in school. Above all, experience teaches.[93] In that sense, all experience could be described as educational.

For present purposes, however, the term is to be understood in the limited sense of the experience of an individual that results from involvement in the formal educational system.

In practice, formal educational effort is directed on one hand to the development of the individual person, and on the other to the needs and wellbeing of the community that provides it.

If the individual's resulting experience leads to the harmonious and integrated development of the whole person, it can properly be called educational. If it is directed principally towards equipping the individal to meet the needs of the community to which he belongs, it should be described as schooling, even although, incidentally, the harmonious development of the whole person may be fostered in some degree.

EDUCATION AND THE COMMUNITY

[Education implies] the concept of citizenship with its implication of allegiance to some form of state.... It covers the accumulated knowledge of a people, about their past, their physical environment ... about the mutual relations of human beings inside and outside the law. It covers their religious beliefs and practices, their ethical codes, their system of values and their philosophical outlook.... These are the vital elements in the cultural traditions of all peoples, whatever their political status, their stage of economic development, whether these elements are enshrined in a literature, or whether in an unwritten form they are preserved in the minds and memories and hearts of a people. These are the roots by which a people lives.[94]

Families are where we discover the bonds of love and trust. Schools are where we learn the collective story of which we are a part. Communities are where we are for other people at times of need, and they for us ... where we ... learn moral literacy, habits of the heart ... the grammar of reciprocity. Community is society with a human face.[95]

Unity of minds and hearts is clearly a universal and deeply-felt wish of humanity. Communities, whether understood as family, city, nation, groups of nations, a civilisation, or the planet, are disunited at every level. If education is to be the catalyst to bring about the desired unity, a beginning has to be made somewhere, preferably at the beginning.

In my end is my beginning. If education does not lead to the harmonious and integrated development of the individual person, there can be little hope that a wider unity will follow.

EDUCATION IN THE REAL WORLD

Can educational experience be directed towards the harmonious development of the community as well as of the individual?

In totalitarian societies, educational systems operated on the basis that education was provided for the benefit of the society, rather than for the subject. In societies said to be free, in which the system is paradoxically based on compulsion, there is a risk that the balance may be tipped in that direction.

In our complex modern society, education/schooling is deemed to be necessary for all persons from five to eighteen years of age, to enable them to conform to the ethos of the society and to contribute to it in so far as in them lies. To help the attainment of the objective, more of the same is on offer at the beginning and end of the process.

The elements necessary for the attainment of this objective are related to society's economic needs, and include such skills as literacy and numeracy, at-one-ness with the physical and human environment, and acceptance of the need for the rule of law.

The elements necessary for subjects to attain their full potential as human beings, in command of themselves and at peace with the universe, fall into another category. For that end, the deepest aspirations of human nature have to be catered for.

It may be that an educational system cannot meet such demands, but at least it should recognise and not suppress or stultify these indefinable longings, 'Reason has to subscribe to a set of affirmations, though they be rationally undemonstrable, because their truth is postulated by the exigencies of moral life.'[96]

Such needs, emotional and spiritual as well as intellectual and physical, aesthetic as well as rational, have to be recognised by the authority which controls and provides the educational process. Their satisfaction will be based on values acceptable because they are necessary for healthy human growth, mentally and spiritually, and are in conformity with the dictates of natural reason.

An education that aims only for the economic prosperity of the community will not be sufficient to foster the kind of mindset in persons that is necessary for them to reach their full potential. Some understanding of human behaviour and of purpose of living has also to be fostered.

This requires a unity of outlook between those who give the education and those who receive it. The absence of this unity may give rise to a system dominated by utilitarian considerations, in which even the first aim, the economic prosperity and survival of the community, will not be furthered.

For a democracy to flourish, its educational system has to aim at forming citizens, willing and able to acquire and assess information, but also to make moral and therefore free judgments, and with the wisdom to achieve the consensus needed to work together for the common good.

The principles, ideas and qualities that are prized in a community, and which define its character and behaviour, that is its fundamental values, have to correspond with those that are necessary for the wellbeing of the individual citizen. Where this congruence is missing an unstable and potentially revolutionary society may result.

FREEDOM AND COMPULSION

Conflict and tensions in individuals and in society are a function of the nature of reality, and are manifest in many different ways – in the conflict between intellect and will,[97] between obedience to the law and freedom of conscience, between self-sacrifice and self-preservation, between contemplation and action. In the educational sphere they are manifest in the polarisation between the needs of the individual and the needs of the community. Ultimately they are the outcome of the dichotomy between the demands of God and of Caesar.

In the Christian educational tradition the way to relieve these tensions and so achieve wholeness, or holiness, was known from the beginning: 'Seek ye first the Kingdom of God, and all things whatsoever will be added to you'. And again: 'He who gains his life must lose it'. The essential element in the search is recognition of the divine element in human beings, and according them the respect appropriate to such a status.[98]

In the past this element was woven into the pedagogical tradition, through its founding in Christian values. Now other cultural strands have entered which are ousting the old. The songs and writings that used to transmit the cultural inheritance from one generation to the next, are disappearing. In this new multicultural society the educational system has to seek a common core of values on which a measure of unity can be founded.

Intellectually, this requires the furthering of an integrated cosmological outlook and a generally acceptable appreciation of the realities of spirit and matter. Spiritually, it requires the advancing of a common view of the nature and dignity of human beings.

In the final analysis it requires that an educational system strikes a balance between a theocentric and an anthropocentric stance. In practice the task of finding and implementing that balance is left at the door of the teacher.

THE TEACHER

The teacher must look towards the goal of human completeness guided by the awareness or divination that assisting in its fulfilment is his task. There is no real teacher who in practice does not believe in the existence of the soul, or in a magic that acts through speech.[99]

Even in this computer-driven age there is no substitute for the teacher. Education is a process which, grappling as it does with the fallout from the profoundly conflictual nature of human society partakes of the nature of war. In the spiritual battle against the powers of ignorance and darkness that is waged perennially at the centre of the educational arena, the front-line troops are the teachers.[100] Their attitudes and behaviour, by commission or omission, consciously or not, have an influence for good or ill on the spiritual and moral development of their pupils.

> Anyone who takes upon himself the responsibility of educating children cannot logically dissociate himself from the practice of moral education.... Since the education of children is crucially a matter of the formation of character, a good teacher ... must also be a virtuous person.... Every teacher is a moral educator.[101]

This belief was enshrined in the Scottish pedagogic tradition, never more elegantly expressed than in Sir James Robertson's pregnant phrase 'Education is the slow commerce of person with person'.[102] It is explicit in the thinking of one of the founding fathers of the modern Scottish system: 'I do not mean to say that it is necessary that a teacher should be a philosopher, but it is quite indispensable that he should philosophise'.[103]

Teachers have to accept and be committed to the ideas and qualities that are prized in the community and which define its character and behaviour, that is its fundamental values, In a united and stable society, these will correspond with those necessary for the wellbeing of the individual citizen.

How to develop freedom of spirit while at the same time commanding obedience to the rule of law is a problem at the heart of all education, which has to be seen as an art of ministering[104] that takes account of the essential nature of the recipient in all its aspects. In the practice of this art educators must aim for wholeness of heart and mind, of body and spirit, in the individual, in conformity if possible with the spiritual outlook of the whole community. They have to be aware of the spiritual unease that afflicts the human condition, and the tensions to which this gives rise, and work towards their amelioration rather than the opposite. It follows that wholeness of heart and mind is a *sine qua non* in the teacher.

During World War Two a serviceman was asked what he would do when he returned to 'civvy-street'. He replied that he would go back to teaching, because there he would know exactly where he would stand in the social pecking order, 'one below the vicar and one above the policeman'.

There was more to his diagnosis of the social order than perhaps he realised. As a teacher it would be his duty to accept and support the moral standards laid down by the ecclesiastical authority, and at the same time instil respect in his pupils for the law of the land. In seeking to satisfy his two masters he would have a recognised place in the social order, and could expect to gain the support and the respect of the community. He was also assuming that the demands would be compatible with one another, and would remain so.

His view of the teaching profession had been formed in a simpler and wiser age, when the teacher's role could be summed up in the phrase 'Guide, philosopher and friend'. It was a 'covenantal relationship, not predicated on interest, but instead on loyalty, fidelity and faithfulness'.[105]

In the post-World War II era, as the period of compulsory schooling lengthened and children reached physical maturity at an ever earlier age, the demands on the teacher changed radically. With the breakdown of family life and an increasing alienation of the young from the mainstream churches, the teacher acquired a subsidiary role, as a kind of intellectual and spiritual midwife, whose task is to deliver the young through an earlier but prolonged adolescence to a delayed adulthood. The school now finds itself asked to fill the space formerly occupied by youth clubs or other voluntary organisations.[106]

In a variety of ways, by the expansion of the area of personal guidance in schools, or by the introduction of sex education into the school curriculum, a part of the role of priest or minister as well as that of parent are being handed to the teacher.

With the lengthening of the period of compulsory schooling, the role of the teacher has to be examined in the varied contexts of pre-school, primary, secondary and tertiary levels. While the need and right of pupils to a degree of freedom of spirit at different stages of development have to be recognised, so also do their corresponding duties. Likewise the limits of the authority which teachers are entitled to exercise have to be made clear, as well as the rights that go along with these duties.

There is a factor which is common to the pupil-teacher relationship in all contexts. It involves the subordination of the teacher's freedom of personal expression to the interests and needs of the pupils. It is in a sense a 'motherly' and even a Christ-like aspect of the role in which the teacher's freedom to develop is sacrificed for the well being of the pupil.

Where that aspect was understood and appreciated by the community at large, the sacrifice of personal development on the part of the teacher was tolerable, and brought its own fulfilment. This was especially so in the case of those bred in the Christian tradition, who accepted that self-abnegation is necessary for everyone. 'He who gains his life must lose it.' When the community no longer acknowledges the necessity of sacrifice, or when the social context has drastically changed, re-appraisal of the teacher's role is urgently needed if the system is not to break down.

It is a further part of the responsibility of the educational system to seek a common core of values able to accommodate the scientific mindset that is at the centre of modern culture. Here the teacher is again at the centre of the action. Is it their function to uphold the wishes of a disparate body of parents, to lead the way to finding common values or to enforce the wishes of a higher authority?

DISCIPLESHIP AND FREEDOM

There remains the question of the willingness of the disciple to follow the master. While the teacher's dictum 'don't do as I do, do as I tell you' has the merit of recognising the difficulties inherent in choosing the path of virtue, it is also a confession of failure. Teachers, who have arrived at their own spiritual convictions by a free act of intellect and will, and accepted that that freedom was necessary for them to do so, must accord the same freedom to their pupils, if they hope to set them on the way to a similar understanding. The fact that pupils are conscripts sets the teacher at a disadvantage from the outset, and gives rise in part to the problem of discipline which all teachers have to face.

From these considerations certain conclusions follow. The first is that the outcome of any educational exercise depends substantially on the teachers who carry it out.

> It is the teacher who will determine whether children have a clear philosophy of life, leading to clear ideas of what is right or wrong. It is the teacher who will give our educational system its bent in the atomic age, and who must find the way to create men fit to live in the new world ahead.[107]

A second conclusion is that the intellectual or spiritual commitment of teachers to the educational philosophy they are imparting, whatever it may be, is a necessary condition for its free and willing acceptance by those taught. Teachers have to be committed to the philosophy or way of life they propagate because they believe it to be true and will lead to the liberation and salvation of their pupils. This is readily seen in an educational system in which a religious faith is integral to its operation.

> The achievement of the school depends not so much on the subject matter or methodology as on the people who work there.... The integration of culture and faith is mediated by the other integration of faith and life in the person of the teacher.[108]

Whatever the philosophical, moral or religious faith on which teachers base their educational practice, it is imperative that they be committed to it. Failure in this regard will render their efforts of no avail. Teachers are inextricably and inevitably involved in the spiritual formation of their pupils. As every teacher knows, and every pupil too, the teacher's fundamental view of the value of the pupil, and of what constitutes goodness, is exposed daily by his or her reaction in response to acts of lying, bullying, justice or injustice, kindness, courage and so on. Neutrality on the part of the teacher in the face of moral decisions has consequences in terms of formation of the pupil, and is not an option. The teacher constantly presents a model of how, or how not, to behave.

> There is no case at all for a morally neutral teacher; he must be seen by his pupils, whatever their age, to be on the side of fairness, honesty and kindness. He cannot be non-judgemental because he is in the judgement seat for most of his working life, especially when his pupils are young, hardly out of the nursery.[109]

If education is an attempt to pass on a view of life or a way of living, success will depend on the extent to which the teacher is seen to live by his or her own philosophy. Even if there is no deliberate attempt to pass on a particular set of values, some kind of view or meaning will be conveyed. Any philosophy, to be true to itself, has to be something more than words; it has to be lived. Philosophical discourse is not the same thing as philosophy.[110] Above all it requires commitment: 'To thine own self be true, and then it follows as the night the day, thou canst not then be false to any man.'

In recent times other powers have usurped the teacher's position as mentor and exemplar in moral matters. The hidden curriculum that has always operated inside and outside the school has been boosted by the potent influence of television and other media. In the ensuing climate the demands on the moral and spiritual reserves of teachers constantly increase while their power effectively to meet new challenges is as constantly diminished.

In any army, those who bear the heat and burden of the day have to be supported by a secondary force of non-combatants, known as staff officers, whose function is to keep the fighting men supplied with everything they require. In a war good staff-work is always necesary, but never sufficient by itself to gain victory. The finest staff-work can not be a substitute for the courage and self-sacrifice called for from front-line troops in the face of the enemy. Poor staff-work, however, can nullify all efforts, and lead to defeat. During the Crimean War, it was said, a consignment of foot-gear for front line troops arrived containing only boots for left feet. Similarly, the lack of suitable clothing for his troops in 1812 contributed to Napoleon's downfall. In the educational war, staff-work is the realm of administrators, governors, inspectors and advisers of all kinds. The front-line troops are parents and teachers In the struggle against the principalities and powers of ignorance and darkness, good organisation and good staff-work, necessary as they are, are never sufficient. Good administration and sound structures cannot of themselves bring forth the desired good fruit; but committed teachers and parents can, and often do, overcome problems due to maladministration and lack of resources, and make poor structures work.

In the aftermath of the Second World War, when strains were showing throughout the educational system, some thought the ills would disappear when restrictions on resources and the endemic shortage of teachers were overcome. Half a century later, when pupil-teacher ratios were generally more advantageous than they had ever been, dissatisfaction inside and outside schools was at an all-time high.

There never have been panaceas in education, and the reduction of class sizes was not one. The fact that it was necessary did not make it sufficient to bring about a cure. The diagnosis was faulty, and something more radical than structural change was needed. Nor was it simply a matter of training, or of techniques in the acquisition and dispensing of knowledge, if teachers and children lacked the tranquillity, stability and commonality of outlook needed for the difficult and demanding action that lies at the heart of every true educational exercise.

In the Scottish system teachers were expected 'to pass on a social and moral inheritance, and direct the sentiments and habits of the young towards the good life.'[111] Whence comes the inheritance, and what constitutes 'good'? The desired enlightenment of the pupil has to be communicated by the teacher through a kind of cultural haze, a spiritual continuum or medium composed of religious, intellectual, socio-economic and administrative elements which have been subjected to continuous, rapid and sometimes traumatic change over many decades. The medium is not the message, but its transparency, or lack of it, affects the transmission of enlightenment as surely as the opacity of any physical medium dims the passage of light. When the Christian ethic was strong in the community and throughout the educational system, a lively consciousness of issues of a moral and spiritual order existed, marked by genuine commitment on the part of teachers to the values of the Christian gospel, and a respect for the worth of persons that flowed from that source. A measure of wholeness was then achieved in the products of the system. In the post-modern, post-post-modern and almost post-Christian society of the *fin de millenium* period and the new age this is no longer so. The crisis in adherence to Christian values has brought about a climate of philosophical confusion inimical to the objectives and transmission of true education.

Needless to say, the crisis is not confined to the schools, nor can the schools themselves effect a cure, no matter how insistent or seductive the cry of education, education, education. Education cannot take place without teachers, who ought to share the responsibility for diagnosis as well as for treatment. They should be able to bring their combined wisdom to bear on the current educational and social malaise. The question is whether they have the unity of outlook and authority to act independently.

GOD AND CAESAR

More than half a century has elapsed since 1945 when the last major shift in educational philosophy took place.

> Human culture is not instinctive. It has to be conquered by a continuous moral effort, which involves the repression of natural instinct and the subordination and sacrifice of the individual impulse to the social purpose. It is the fundamental error of the modern hedonist to believe that man can abandon moral effort and throw off every repression and spiritual discipline and yet preserve all the achievements of culture. It is the lesson of history that the higher the achievement of a culture the greater

is the moral effort and the stricter the social discipline that it demands.[112]

Who can provide the philosophical underpinning the national education system requires to restore the balance between the things of God and of Caesar? Teachers clearly have a part to play in such an enterprise. In practice, like mothers, they are carried along by the overwhelming immediate demands on their energy by their charges, without the freedom needed to assess and re-direct the educational effort. Those who are devoted to the preservation of Christian values, whether in the denominational sector or not, see the solution of the perennial difficulties of educating the young in the context of the restoration of the Christian tradition. In practice, however, they are subject to two masters, or perhaps to two philosophies, and are unable completely to satisfy either.

The inevitable tension can be eased only if there is a degree of convergence in the demands imposed by their masters. This will require an appreciation on the part of Caesar of the benefits to the common good of a sound moral philosophy and therefore of the foundations on which moral teaching or witness can be based; and on the part of the Church, recognition of the degree of authority the teacher needs if his or her message is to be credible.

The following is a quotation from a lecture delivered in 1943 while World War II was still being waged:

If mankind overcomes the terrible threats of slavery and dehumanisation which it faces today, it will thirst for a new humanism, and be eager to rediscover the integrity of man.... What will assume full importance for tomorrow are the vital connections of man with society, that is, not only the social environment but also common work and common good.... Education must develop the sense of freedom and the sense of responsibility, human rights and human obligations, authority for the general welfare and respect for the humanity of each individual person.... Education must bring an end to the cleavage between religious inspiration and secular activity ... between work or useful activity and the blossoming of spiritual life and disinterested joy in knowledge and beauty ... everyone must work, or share in the burden of social community ... but work is not an end in itself; it should afford leisure for the joy, expansion and delight of the spirit. Education must provide the common man with means for his personal fulfilment, not only with regard to his labour but also to his social and political activities and to his leisure.[113]

In this quotation, for 'education', substitute 'teachers'. Then ask, 'who will teach the teachers?'

7

Doing Without God

It is in losing God that man has lost his reason: he will not find it again without having first found God again.

Étienne Gilson, *The Terrors of the Year 2000*[114]

As the Second Millenium was drawing to its close, the Christian traditions of the industrialised and urbanised western world that informed its educational systems were eroding, and the implicit moral sanctions losing their force. For the teacher of the Third Millenium, the need arises of finding a substitute in a system which tries to do without God, or some equally effective transcendent principle.

In 1949 Gilson, a distinguished Neo-Thomist philosopher, foreseeing a world without faith in anything other than human intelligence and energy, wrote a prose-poem from which the above quotation is taken. In it he compares the mental set of the people of the year 948, who were expecting the Antichrist to appear at the end of the first millenium, with that of the people of 1948, still in shock after Hiroshima, who were being told by philosophers that God was dead.

From 1914 to 1918, the world was ravaged by a war which had known no parallel. A mighty people broke through its boundaries and spread over Europe, leaving in its wake ruins past numbering, dead by the millions, and historical materialism, master of Holy Russia, whence later we have seen it menacing the whole earth. Even during that armistice of twenty years which we took for peace, what tragic bloodshed! China in perpetual war seems a little far away for us to worry about what happens there, but have we already forgotten what took place during that barbarous civil war in Most Christian Spain, where man was so cruel to man that those who saw it lower their voices to speak of it, and murmur: 'Anything, rather than see that again!' The tenth century famine? But I have only to shut my eyes for a moment to see once more, in the villages of the Ukraine and on the banks of the Volga, the dead children in 1922, whose little corpses lay abandoned in their emptied schools; or again, wandering along the railways, those bands of children reduced to savagery who later were to be mowed down with machine guns. At the beginning of the twentieth century, as at the end of the tenth – official documents bear witness to the fact parents devoured their offspring. Fathers and mothers like our own, like ourselves, but who knew the meaning of that frightful word: hunger.

That, however was but a modest beginning. We saw the German army hurled upon Europe a second time, like a great tidal wave; Poland vanquished, plundered, butchered; nations falling one after the other under the blows of an irresistible conqueror. France in agony, her very honour wounded. Paris crumbles in its turn, and the echo of its downfall reverberates in the silence of an astonished world. A Raoul Glaber of the year Two Thousand would never stop multiplying the chapters of this woeful tale. He would have to describe the prodigious series of disasters which now swoop down upon the entire world and to which we ourselves, who witnessed them, can scarcely bear testimony. The sky everywhere furrowed by fiery dragons much more formidable than those which, on the threshold of the year One Thousand, crossed from north to south the sky of France; in Japan, in the South Sea Islands, in China, in Russia, in Germany, in France, in Italy – in that very England which believed itself sheltered behind our army, its fleet and the depths of its surrounding seas – a heap of ruins which has not yet been cleared away and which is there for us to see; the numbers of dead increase and they are still in our hearts for us to mourn; a whole race condemned to destruction, savagely wiped out, pursued by a hatred fierce and ingenious as only man is capable of conceiving for man. Germany opened for the Jews, and closed upon them, charnel pits whose numbers we still do not know. Of course, all this was to be brought to a close by a liberation, but we know what further details and further ruins this was to cost, even to that bomb of Hiroshima, whose solemn detonation announced to a terrified world, with the supposed close of a war which peace has yet followed, the dawn of a new era where science, formerly our hope and our joy, would be the source of greatest terror.

Man has just made the most outstanding of his discoveries, but by a symbolism the more striking for being quite involuntary, the great secret that science has just wrested from matter is the secret of its destruction. To know today is synonymous with to destroy. Nuclear fission is not only the most intimate revelation of the nature of the physical world and the freeing of the most powerful energy that has ever been held, but at the same time and inevitably the most frightful agent of destruction which man has ever had at his disposal. The three are inseparable. Atomic piles can be built more and more powerful, and immense quantities of useful energy can thus be produced, but the operation of these piles yields as a by-product the very explosive of the atom bomb. Not only does man know today so many things that he wonders if he will be able to control his own domination, but the conditions of his rule are such that they present to the scientist this tragic dilemma: formerly, it was by obeying her that one mastered nature, now it is by destroying her.

And yet we are only at the beginning. The age of atomic physics will see the birth of a new world, as different from our own as ours is from the world before steam and electricity. Doubtless, it will be even more so for things will move quickly – especially when to the era of physics there will succeed the still more redoubtable one of biology. Very few of those who work in laboratories doubt it: we are on the verge of a great mystery which may, any day, surrender its secret. We will be able to work, not only on inert matter, but even on life, and it is not only the breadth of our power but its very nature which will become terrifying; and the more so that here again, and for the same reason, the possibility of good is inseparable from that of evil.

Pasteurian arms is today a common term. It is a horrible term, and it carries with it a symbolism that is more impressive because it is entirely independent of all human intention. Pasteur never cultivated microbes except to attenuate the virulence of their cultures, and thus save human lives. Today, on the contrary, we are striving to increase their virulence in order to kill and no longer to cure. The biology of tomorrow will allow more subtle, but not the less formidable, interventions in human destiny. Can we imagine the repercussions which the free determination of the sexes will have some day, perhaps in the near future? Can we picture what would happen in a world where we could not only turn out males and females at will, but select them and produce human beings adapted to various functions as do breeders with dogs or horses or cattle? In that future society which will know how to give itself the slaves and even the reproducers which it needs, what will become of the liberty and dignity of the human person? For once, the most daring prophecies of H. G. Wells appear tame, for in *The Island of Dr Moreau* they were still only working to transform wild brutes into men; in the future society, it is men whom they will be transforming into brutes – to use them to foster the ends of a humanity thenceforth unworthy of the name.

And these are not today – as in 948 – fears localised in a small corner of the earth. It is a world-wide terror, with the whole planet as its domain, from Vladivostock around the world to Alaska, by way of Moscow, Berlin, Paris, London and Washington. But do we really know its cause?

These men of the tenth century knew at least what they feared.

Not at all – as has been erroneously reiterated – the end of the world, but an event which, on the contrary, was to precede it by a sufficiently long interval of time which was announced prophetically in the Apocalypse, ch. 20, v. 7: 'Then, when the thousand years are over, Satan will be let loose from his prison, and will go out to seduce the nations that live at the four corners of the earth – that is the meaning of Gog and Magog – and muster them for battle, countless as the sand by the sea'. That is the way St. John himself had said it, the enemy of God was soon to appear, ushering in a fearful era of abomination and desolation.

By what signs would we recognize it? The question was asked with that curiosity which always tempers anxiety; and moreover the Middle Ages had on that point precisions that surprise us a little. The Beast with seven heads and ten horns was Satan 'and the names it bore on its heads were names of blasphemy', which the Apocalypse describes: like a leopard, but it had bear's feet and a lion's mouth. A secret number formulates his essence, and 'let the reader, if he has the skill, cast up the sum of the figures in the beast's name, after our human fashion, and the number will be six hundred and sixty-six'. Why? It is, as St Irenaeus says, that Noah was six hundred years old at the time of the flood, the statue of Nabuchodonosor was sixty cubits high and six cubits wide: add the age of Noah and the height and width of the statue of Nabuchodonosor and you get six hundred and sixty-six. This is not only clear, it is evident! Would you know his name? Evanthas, Lateinos, Titan, perhaps another. Irenaeus knows everything. He even informs us that the Antichrist will devastate the whole earth, reigning in the Temple three years and three months; and after that will come the end of the world when creation will have lasted six thousand years.

Today we cannot read these details without at first an amused smile on our lips. On that subject the Bishop of Lyons knows so many things, that the future unfolds before him with all the regulated precision of the scenario of a super-film. We ourselves enter into the spirit of the thing and put a few questions to him, but he has an answer for everything. Why should the world last exactly six thousand years? It is because creation lasted six days and since a day of creation is worth a thousand years, the world will come to an end after the six days of creation have run their course. The answer is perfect! But here we stop smiling and an uncomfortable doubt slips into our mind. Six thousand years? But how old was the world at the time of Christ? Suppose the six thousand years of the world were not finally to have expired until around the year Two Thousand? The scourges which have struck us, the menace of the blows which await us, do not favour abandoning this hypothesis. If the drama which we live does not announce the end of the world, it is a rather good dress rehearsal. Shall we see worse than Buchenwald, Lydice and Oradour-sur-Glane? Perhaps it is not impossible, but it is difficult to believe. At this point in our reflections, we cast our eyes about and ask anxiously: 'But where is Antichrist?' And behold, he is right there! Ecce homo, said Friedrich Neitzche of himself: behold the man! This time, no longer God who becomes man to make him divine, but man who makes himself God to usurp his place and who wishes to be his own god. We are surprised at first, for he bears no resemblance to the fantastic beast of the Apocalypse. However, like it he has a number, and it is a human number. On the body of a man, a man's head with a hard, wilful chin, a broad intellectual forehead crowned with blasphemies, and in his beautiful eyes the anguish of insanity. His name is none of those which they had told us. He does not call himself Lateinos, Evanthas but Zarathustra, and behold he speaks like the one of whom St. Paul formerly prophesied, who will go so far as to sit 'in God's temple, and proclaim himself as God'. (II Thess. ii, 4).

That is indeed what Nietzche does, when he puts himself forward as the sole guardian of the terrifying explosive which humanity does not yet know and which will nevertheless change its destiny. More powerful than the bomb of Hiroshima which it prefigures, and a thousand times more devastating still, the terrifying message that Zarathustra murmurs to himself as he comes towards us is contained in these few very simple words:

'They do not know that God is dead'. He himself, at least, I know it, and that is why his name is Ante-christus as well as Anti-christus. 'Have you understood me?' he asks. 'Dionysus face to face with the Crucifix.' He does not only come before Christ but against Him.

This is the capital discovery of modern times, the event of which all the rest, tragic as they may be, are only the corollaries or the sequels. Trace back as far as you like the history of humanity and you will find no upheaval to compare with this in the extent or in the depth of its cause. The demoniac grandeur of Nietzsche is that he does know and that he says so. This is not just our imagination; it is enough to read his *Ecce Homo* to have proof of it: 'I know my fate. A day will come when the remembrance of a fearful event will be fixed to my name, the remembrance of a unique crisis in the history of the earth, of the most profound clash of consciences, of a decree enacted against all that had been believed, exacted and sanctified right down to our days. I am not a man, I am dynamite'. Do you doubt for an instant that he would have said today 'an atomic bomb'? And how right he is! From his very beginning, man had thought nothing, said nothing, done nothing that did not draw its inspiration from this certitude that there existed a God or god. And behold, all of a sudden, there is no longer one, or rather, we see that there never was one! We shall have to change completely our every thought, word and deed. The entire human order totters on its base. Antichrist is still the only one who knows this, the only one who foresees the appalling cataclysm of the 'reversal of values' which is in the making, for if the totality of the human past depended on the certitude that God exists, the totality of its future must needs depend on the contrary certitude, that God does not exist. But see the folly of men who do not yet know this, or who continue to act as if two or three among them did not know it already! Everything that was true from the beginning of the human race will suddenly become false, but what will become true? Whether he knows it or not, man alone must create for himself a new formula of life, which will be that of his destiny.

Very well, let us get to work. But man will never use his creative liberty as long as he believes that what is already dead is still living. Nietzsche has definite knowledge of his mission to destroy: 'When truth opens war on the age-old falsehood, we shall witness upheavals unheard of in the history of the world, earthquakes will twist the earth, the mountains and the valleys will be displaced, and everything hitherto imaginable will be surpassed. Politics will then be completely absorbed by the war of ideas and all the combinations of power of the old society will be shattered since they are all built on falsehood: there will be wars such as the earth will never have seen before. It is only with me that great politics begin on the globe ... I know the intoxicating pleasure of destroying to a degree proportionate to my power of destruction'.

Have we understood at last? That is not certain, because the announcement of a cataclysm of such magnitude ordinarily leaves but a single escape: to disbelieve it and, in order not to believe, to refuse to understand it. If Nietzsche speaks truly, it is the very foundations of human life which are to be overthrown. Before stating what will be true, we will have to say that everything by which man has thus far lived, everything by which he still lives, is deception and trickery. 'He who would be a creator, both in good and evil, must first of all know how to destroy and to wreck values.' They are, in fact, being wrecked around us, and under our very feet, everywhere. We have stopped counting the unheard of theories thrown at us under names as various as their methods of thought, each the harbinger of a new truth which it promises to create shortly, joyously busy preparing the brave new world of tomorrow by first of all annihilating the world of today.

Destroying today to create tomorrow, such is indeed the mission of the seducer. 'I am the first immoralist, I am thereby the destroyer par excellence.' He knows his mission, and his disciples too have understood it. It is not only to some of their novels, it is to their entire work that *The Immoralist* of Gide would serve as a rather good title. That is merely literature? Doubtless, and it is sometimes beautiful – but have we not long known that the seducer would be handsome? That we should not have foreseen him, is still forgivable. But that we should not understand what he is doing while he is doing it right under our eyes, just as we were told he would do it – that bears witness to a stranger blindness. Can it really be that the herd of human beings that is being led to slaughter has eyes and yet does not see?

It is none the less very simple! Whatever criticism can be levelled at the venerable Artisan of the Bible, let us at least do him the justice of admitting that he knew quite well what 'to create' means. He did not take himself for some Greek demigod, fashioning to his idea a material which did not owe him existence. Insofar as a thing is made out of another, concession must be made to the material which is used. To create, on the contrary, is truly to make something of nothing, in the supreme freedom of an act which, since it is producing *ex nihilo*, nothing conditions, nothing determines, nothing limits. A truly gratuitous act of which one is the sole and complete author, that is the only act which is truly creative because it alone is truly free. In an eternity which transcended time, Jehovah was free; but we are not, for even if the world was not created, everything appears to us as if it had been created, for it exists. And it is indeed that world which restricts us! Try as we may to fashion it and remodel it, in a hundred different ways, we shall only make of it what its nature allows us to make. We shall perhaps be great manufacturers, but creators – never! To create in his turn *ex nihilo*, man must first of all re-establish everywhere the void.

It is too soon yet to create, but one can begin to destroy. Man is thus occupied on all sides with that intoxicating joy which Nietzsche has just told us is as great as his power of destruction. Perhaps that is the answer to the poignant question which so many of us are asking ourselves: what does man want? Has he gone mad? Yes, in a sense, but only with the supremely lucid madness of a creature who would annihilate the obstacle which being places in the way of his creative ambitions. Such is the profound sense of our solemn and tragic adventure. Antichrist is not among us, he is in us. It is man himself, usurping unlimited creative power and proceeding to the certain annihilation of that which is, in order to clear the way for the problematic creation of what will be.

We are then in the decisive moment of a cosmic drama. Quis ut Deus? It is I, says man. When we no longer want to be the image of God, we still can be his caricature! The explosion of Hiroshima did not only silence that atrocious clamour which swelled towards us from the camps of slow death and the charnel pits of Germany, it will resound for a long time, as a solemn assertion with a definite meaning. We have at last seen through the secret of matter! We know exactly how it is made, since we are able to destroy it. How will the world end? We used to think we knew; then science accustomed us to consider these answers as myths, and behold it now produces its own answer. On the threshold of a new millennium, man has the proud conviction that the day is perhaps not far off when he himself will be able to explode the planet. Let us admit that the adventure is enticing. You press a button, and the earth bursts like a gigantic bomb whose pulverized fragments are lost in a shower or stars which the startled eyes of the Martians – if there be any – will see shooting through the night into space. As a child who amuses himself by breaking his toy for no reason at all, just to see what it is like inside, so man will have smashed the world. It is possible that another will then be born, but that is not certain; in the meantime, what is certain is that ours will be ended.

At least, it will be said, man is free! One can henceforth attempt all things, and especially in the realm of the mind. So wrote Stephane Mallarme, whose whole work attests what has been called 'the obsession to abolish', but who would abolish everything only that he himself might perform a pure act of creation and thus, as it has been said, 'became equal to God'. Is not that precisely the sacrilegious effort whose meaning we would like to decipher? The terms which a critic of Mallarme used to describe his poetic enterprise fit exactly the mad ambitions of modern man: 'to construct a poetry which would have the value of a preternatural creation and which would be able to enter into rivalry with the world of created things to the point of supplanting it totally'.

To abolish existing creation in order to create another: that is also the ambition of authentic surrealism, by which I mean the one which Andre Breton defined a short while ago as: 'something dictated by thought, released from all control of reason, divorced from all aesthetic or moral preoccupation'. We will then be able to say everything as well as to do everything. If we start by annihilating everything, what limits can stop us? None whatever. Everything is possible, provided only that this creative spark which surrealism seeks to disclose deep in our being be preceded by a devastating flame. 'The most simple surrealist act consists in this: to go down into the streets, pistol in hand, and shoot at random, for all you are worth, into the crowd.' Why not? This massacre of values is necessary to create values that are really new. 'Everything is still to be done', affirms Andre Breton, 'every means becomes good when employed to destroy the ideas of family, native land, religion.' Now that is not only necessary: since God is dead, it has become possible. The eternal obstructor who has encumbered the heavens ever since the beginning of the world has suddenly disappeared. The terrible interlocutor to whom, during ages without number, man gave only trembling reply – behold he has suddenly vanished, leaving for the first time man, face to face with himself, alone in a world empty of God, and at last master of his destiny. 'But, Smerdiakof', says old Karamazov, 'if God does not exist, then everything is permitted.' What a prodigious liberation! Man knows henceforward that he can do anything without the echo in his ear of the redoubtable summons of the sovereign judge, 'Adam, where art thou?' There is no longer any judge, save Adam himself, who, since he alone makes the law, alone applies it, without knowing yet that man is for himself the hardest of masters and that, by a comparison with the yoke which he lays on his own shoulders, that of the Lord was light to bear.

To learn this, he needs a bit of time. Long after the amazing discovery that all is henceforth permitted, man still continues to act as if that which had formerly been forbidden still remained so. The ancient law of good and evil continues to rule his actions, but instead of being called the divine law it is called the voice of conscience. Nothing has then been gained, and man has merely changed the name of his master; until the inevitable day when conscience, finding herself but the lees of long use, doubts in her turn that even she has authority to impose law. It is only then that all becomes actually permissible, and to the question: what must we do?, there is no longer an answer, but from the moment when there is no longer anything that man must do, he no longer knows what he will do. As the soldier, on leave, knows the desolation of twenty-four hours passed with nothing to do, man knows today that infinitely more tragic desolation of a life which is all spent in the idleness of a liberty he is powerless to use.

It is this nausea that has engendered contemporary existentialism and, we must admit, its courageous decision to dispel it. 'Existentialism', says Sartre, 'is nothing other than an effort to draw all the consequences from a coherently atheistic position.' That is true, and these consequences are terrible. Everything is permissible if God does not exist, but also, as a consequence, man is abandoned, for he finds neither within nor without himself anything on which to rely. Then begins for him the stern martyrdom of the paths of liberty. 'We have neither behind us nor before us, in the bright domain of values, any justification or excuse. We are alone, without excuse. That is what I would express in saying that man is condemned to be free … man, without any support and without any help, is condemned at each moment to invent man.' A truly exhausting task, that of a perpetual invention of self, without model, without purpose, without rule. The father of existentialism is not Prometheus bound, nor even unbound, but rather Sisyphus, 'the hero of the absurd'. Tragic hero, because he knows, and by that very fact is superior to his destiny. Is he not stronger than his rock, asks Albert Camus, since he rolls it eternally? 'To live is to make the absurd live. To make it live is above all to contemplate it.'

That the absurd creates itself out of nothing is not astonishing, nor that it nauseates him. But these are the sports of the princes of the mind. For unless we welcome the eerie invitation to suicide, our problem is to live. A half-dozen intellectuals may find a meaning for the absurd in the literary success they gain by it, but such a justification has no value for the masses of ordinary men, liberated by atheism and who, having become gods without asking for it, do not know what to do with their divinity. The latter make no pretence to save themselves, they eagerly beg to be saved. Then there appear other men who undertake to exploit atheism in their turn, and who organize the cult of the new god. It is not without a profound philosophical reason that Marxism required atheism as one of its necessary principles.

'Aragon and I', Andre Breton used to write. Let us not be surprised that Aragon, a Marxist writer, made his debut under the chief of the surrealists. Their paths have since parted, but all the creative ambitions of the man who makes himself god at least find a harmony in the will to destroy which they presuppose. How could Marxism be able truly to free man, if it did not first free him of God? Since Feuerbach, we know exactly what is the essence of Christianity and how man, who believed himself the creature of God, is on the contrary His creator. Since there is no longer anything between man and himself, there is no longer anything between man and other men. Once again, he is free, but is he truly free? Once he is free of God, he is no longer free of other men, between whom and himself there never existed any other protection but God and the law of God. It is a very old story. We read in the Book of judges (xxi, 24): 'In those days there was no king in Israel: but everyone did that which seemed right to himself'. The day came, however, when this free people grew tired of its liberty, and as the prophet Samuel was growing old, they went to him and said: 'Make us a king, to judge us, as all nations have'. At these words, Samuel experienced a great sadness, for he thought he had always judged according to the law of God, but he feared he had committed some fault and by it had turned men from that law.

The Lord knew his thoughts, and said to him: 'Hearken to the voice of the people in all that they say to thee. For they have not rejected thee, but me, that I should not reign over them'. However, before granting the Jewish people the king that they asked, God made known to them the rights that their future masters would not fail to claim: 'He will take your sons and put them in his chariots, and will make them his horsemen, and his running footmen to run before his chariots. And he will appoint of them to plough his fields, and to reap his corn, and to make him arms and chariots. Moreover, he will take the tenth of your corn to give to his servants'. We have seen these things and worse still, for if governments today were satisfied with an income tax of ten percent, what a sigh of relief would we hear in the world! Since men have refused to serve God, there is no longer an arbiter between them and the State which dominates them. It is no longer God, it is the State which judges them. But who, then, will judge the State?

To know the answer to this, it is enough to glance at what is going on round about us. To judge the State, there is no one left. In every land and in all countries, the people wait with fear and trembling for the powerful of this world to decide their lot for them. They hesitate, uncertain, among the various forms of slavery which are being prepared for them. Listening with bated breath to the sounds of those countries which fall one after the other with a crash followed by a long silence, they wonder in anguish how long will last this little liberty they still possess. The waiting is so tense that many feel a vague consent to slavery secretly germinating within themselves. With growing impatience, they await the arrival of the master who will impose on them all forms of slavery, starting with the worst and most degrading of all – that of the mind. Blessed be he who will deliver us from ourselves! Alone under a heaven henceforth empty, man offers to whoever is willing to take it, this futile liberty which he does not know how to use. He is ready for all the dictators, leaders of these human herds who follow them as guides and who are all finally conducted by them to the same place – the abattoir.

What, then, is to be done? To this question permit me to reply by another: In this year of grace, 1948, how much grace is there still left? And this would be the whole question if there did not remain a second one: Is man willing to receive what still remains of grace today? For it is not by wallowing in the evil but in turning our backs on its cause that the remedy can be found. Let us not say: it is too late, and there is nothing left to do; but let us have the courage to look for the evil and the remedy where they exist. It is in losing God that man has lost his reason: he will not find it again without having first found God again.

There was in the thirteenth century a philosopher to whom the sight of the world did not give nausea, but a joy ever new, because he saw in it only order and beauty. Man did not seem to him a Sisyphus hopelessly condemned to the liberty of the absurd, for he read in his own heart the clear law of practical reason. On all sides, within as well as Without, a single and self-same light enlightens the understanding and regulates things, for the spirit which is found in them reconstructs them in the mind according to the order of the same creative intelligibility. This harmony of thought and reality which in our time Einstein describes as the most incomprehensible of mysteries, does not astonish our philosopher, for he knows its source – that same God Whose pure existence is at the origin of all reality as well as of all knowledge. And what is liberty for created man, unless it be to accept himself lovingly, even as his Creator wants and loves him? What is it to act as a free man unless it be to regulate the will according to reason, and reason itself according to the divine law? The vastest community is the universe. God, Who created it, governs it according to the eternal law, of which the natural law, the human and the moral law are only so many particular expressions. Not a sin, not a moral fault is there which is not first of all an error made to the detriment of intelligible light, in violation of the laws of the supreme reason.

Eminently habitable, because it is Christian, is this universe of St Thomas Aquinas still ours? I am afraid not. It is, however, the only one in which man can live without having to create himself in the permanent anguish of his own nothingness, without having eternally to push up again and again the rock of Sisyphus or to yield to the fascination of a slavery which will deliver him even from the memory of liberty. This world is that of the divine wisdom which penetrates everything with its power and orders all with sweetness. Raoul Glaber reports that after so many misfortunes and fateful presages, a sort of peace came into the heavens and the earth was covered with a white robe of churches. Thus disappeared the fears of the year One Thousand. Salvation is the same today. There still remains only God to protect man against man. Either we will serve Him in spirit and in truth, or we shall enslave ourselves ceaselessly, more and more, to the monstrous idol which we have made with our own hands to our own image and likeness. The cause of so many miseries is indeed the ignorance which men have of an important message: they no longer know that a Saviour is born to us. This is not the message of Zarathustra, it is the promise of peace which rang out, nearly two thousand years ago, in the skies of Bethlehem.

He that has eyes to see, let him see. Can it be doubted that there is substance in Gilson's prophecy, or denied that values have been or are being massacred on a global scale?

However, all is not lost. In 1946 Aldous Huxley pointed to the fact that human intuition can be perceptive enough to find the way to salvation:

Knowledge is a function of being. When there is a change in the being of the knower, there is a corresponding change in the nature and amount of knowing. It is a fact, confirmed and reconfirmed during two or three thousand years of religious history, that the ultimate reality is not clearly and immediately apprehended, except by those who have made themselves loving, pure in heart and poor in spirit.[115]

More recently, Pope John Paul II wrote of the possibility of finding the way out of the moral maze:

In order to set contemporary man free from fear of himself, of the world, of others, of earthly powers, of oppressive systems, in order to set him free from every manifestation of a servile fear before that 'prevailing force' that believers call God, it is necessary to pray fervently that he will bear and cultivate in his heart that true fear of God, which is the beginning of wisdom. This fear of God is the saving power of the Gospel. Andre Malraux was right when he said that the twenty-first century would be the century of religion or it would not be at all.[116]

Sursum corda. In whatever role Christian educators bear witness to their Faith in Education, whether as 'parents', 'guides', 'ministers' or 'cosmologists'; they should take heart. 'There must be a close and infinitely significant relationship between Christ and the evolving cosmos' which has to be the source of our continuing faith in education.[117]

Endnotes

1 T.C. Smout, *A History of the Scottish People 1560-1830* (1969) 421.

2 Advisory Council on Education in Scotland, *Secondary Education: A Report of the Advisory Council on Education in Scotland* (London, 1947).

3 John Milton, *L'Allegro.*

4 See also Golding, *The Lord of the Flies.*

5 Leader in *The Times*, 13 June 1996.

6 R.D. Anderson, *Education and Opportunity in Victorian Scotland* (1983).

7 E. Gilson, *The Unity of Philosophical Experience* (1938).

8 In the Preamble to the Parliamentary Education Acts of 1945.

9 O. Chadwick, *The Secularisation of the European Mind in the Nineteenth Century* (1975).

10 'With the foundation of the Welfare State … Britain reached almost the end of the road. From that time on, material welfare was divorced from spiritual welfare, and religion seemed at once to become a matter of private taste. Yet historically … providing support and care for those in need had been … exclusively the work of the churches and those motivated by religion.' B. McSweeney, *Roman Catholicism* (1980). See also R.H. Tawney, *Protestantism and the Rise of Capitalism* (London, 1937) xiv: 'Puritanism helped to mould the social order, but was also itself increasingly moulded by it'.

11 See D. Hay, *Exploring inner space: Is God still possible in the Twentieth Century?* (Oxford, 1987).

12 P. Zind, *Les Nouvelles Congrégations de Frères Enseignant en France de 1800-1830* (1969) 465 ff.

13 'Honour thy father and thy mother' (Exodus 20:12 KJV).

14 'Man is not a mind that thinks, but a being who knows other beings as true, who loves them as good, and who enjoys them as beautiful.' 'To love wisdom is also to love science, and prudence; it

is to seek peace in the inner accord of each mind with itself and in the mutual accord of all minds.' E. Gilson, *The Unity of Philosophical Experience*, 323, 327.

15 *Gaudium et Spes*, 61.

16 Cardinal Hume, in an address to the Catholic Children's Society, quoted in *The Tablet*, 6 July 1991.

17 C. Dawson, *Enquiries* (1933) 273.

18 'In all human societies moral and tradition and law decree that the group consisting of a woman and her offspring is not a socially complete unit ... the human family must consist of the male as well as the female.' B. Malinowski, *Sex and Repression in Savage Society,* quoted by Dawson in *Enquiries*, 271. 'If we let go our respect for marriage, how can we keep our families together, rear the children and look after the sick and old? Marriage is like the magnetic north on the compass – with it you know where you are heading, without it our community would fall apart.' Irish travelling women, quoted in *The Tablet*, 4 November 1995, 1405.

19 J. Dominian, *The Tablet*, 6 February 1999, 162.

20 Cardinal Winning.

21 Quoted in Cruickshank, *History of the Training of Teachers in Scotland* (1970) 96.

22 *The Herald*, 15 November 1995. The then Bishop Holloway of the Scottish Episcopal Church commented, 'People are forced to find appropriate rules for their own culture that reflect their needs, knowledge and understanding. The Bible is still a useful guide but we have to recognise it is a creature of its time. This is particularly true of its moral systems'.

23 Scottish Education Department, Millar Report (1972).

24 Scottish Education Department, *Guidance in Scottish Secondary Schools*, Section 19.

25 Second Vatican Council, *Declaration on Christian Education* (*Gravissimum Verbum*), 639–40.

26 W. Moberley, *The Crisis in the University* (1949) 69.

27 Advisory Report on Secondary Education (2005) Section 90, 17.

28 O. Chadwick, *The Secularisation if the European Mind in the Nineteenth Century*, 232.

29 The method of Dr Suzuki in the teaching of young children to play the violin is illuminating in this respect.

30 T. C. Smout (1969) 432.

31 T. A. FitzPatrick, *Catholic Secondary Education in South West Scotland before 1972* (1986) 30–1.

32 R. Scruton, *The Intelligent Person's Guide to Modern Culture* (2000).

33 S.E.D., *Documents on Religious and Moral Education* (1995) 5–14, 5.

34 *Guidance in Scottish Secondary Schools*, Scottish Education Department, (Edinburgh, 1968) 9.

35 *Curriculum and Assessment in Scotland: A Policy for the 90s* (Edinburgh, 1999) 2.

36 Rousseau, *Profession of Faith of a Savoyard Vicar* (1889), 64.

37 J. Scotland and I. C. M. Fairweather (eds), *A Good Education* (1982).

38 E. Gilson, 238.

39 O. Chadwick, 230.

40 Millar Report, sec. 3.13, 43.

41 P. Zind, *Les Nouvelles Congrégations de Frères Enseignant en France de 1800-1830*, 226ff.

42 I. Murdoch, *Metaphysics as a Guide to Morals* (1992) 481.

43 M. Warnock, *A Common Policy for Education* (Oxford, 1988).

44 J. Scotland and I. C. M. Fairweather, 35.

45 John Paul II, *Veritatis Splendor* (London, 1993).

46 Hans Kung in the Gresham Special Lecture, 'A Global Ethic for the New Millenium', St Paul's Cathedral, 9 May 2000.

47 C. Harvie, *No Gods and Precious Few Heroes: Scotland 1914–1980* (1981).

48 J. Cornwell, *Strange Gods* (New York, 1993). 'Thou shalt not have strange gods before me', Exodus 20:3 (Douai-Rheims).

49 John Paul II, *Fides et Ratio* (London, 1998) 27.

50 'The pupil's search after truth in any subject is capable of including a religious dimension.' *Proposals for a Core Syllabus in Religious Education in Grant-aided schools in Northern Ireland*, The Churches' Religious Education Core Syllabus Drafting Group (1991) 7.

51 *The Tablet*, 06 October 2007, 25.

52 A. Einstein, 'Science and Religion' *Nature* (1940).

53 'Science, Art and Religion' in T. Honderich, *The Oxford Companion to Philosophy*, 813.

54 G. Steiner, *Real Presences* (1989) 225.

55 John Paul II, *Veritatis Splendor*, 4.

56 Cardinal Hume, quoted in *The Tablet*, 21 July 1990.

57 O. Chadwick, 241–2

58 Hans Kung, *Why I am still a Christian*.

59 A Cabbalist rabbi, quoted by Rabbi Blue in *The Tablet*, 13 May 2000, 639.

60 John Paul II, *Fides et Ratio*, 1413-4.

61 *Proposals for a Core Syllabus in Religious Education in Grant-aided schools in Northern Ireland*, 5.

62 *Commitment and Neutrality in Religious Education*, 90.

63 W. Storrar, *Scottish Identity – A Christian Vision* (1990) 10.

64 Cardinal Hume at Newman College Birmingham, quoted in *The Tablet*, 6 July 1991.

65 R. Ullich, discussing the thought of Clement of Alexandria, in *History of Religious Education* (1968) 39–41.

66 Documents of the Second Vatican Council, *Gaudium et Spes*, 61.

67 'There can be no peace in the world unless there is peace between the great religions', Hans Kung, quoted in J. D. Beversluis, *Sourcebook of the World Religions* (Novato, 2000) 159. 'A Religious Studies approach, whereby pupils are asked to attempt an objective study of Christianity or of another religion, has a valuable place in the religious education of adolescents, for GCSE or A level examinations.' *Religious Education in Northern Ireland*, 6.

68 Documents of Vatican II, *Gaudium et Spes*, 62.

69 A. N. Whitehead, *Science and the Modern World*, (1938) 30–1.

70 Documents of Vatican II, *Gaudium et Spes*, 61.

71 Pope John Paul II, *Fides et Ratio*, 34.

72 British monk (c. 354–420/440) who denied the doctrine of Original Sin and held to an interpretation of the freedom of the Will vigorously opposed by Saint Augustine, among others.

73 'When approval was sought for the founding of a Catholic Teacher Training College at Dowanhill in 1894, permission was given on condition that adequate provision be made for the teaching of science'. T. A. Fitzpatrick, *No Mean Service* (1995) 34–5, 43.

74 Sir James Jeans, *The Mysterious Universe*. The first edition was reprinted six times, and the second twice before the first cheap edition, price two shillings, appeared in 1932, 110,000 copies had already been sold.

75 John D. Barrow, *Impossibility: The Limits of Science and the Science of Limits* (Oxford, 1998).

76 John Paul II, quoted in *The Tablet*, 10 October 1987.

77 Preface to the second edition of Newton's *Principia* (1713).

78 From my notes of a Gifford Lecture by Geoffrey Cantor, Glasgow March 1988.

79 E. T. Whittaker, 'Aristotle, Newton, Einstein' (1942).

80 Louis MacNeice, 'Star-gazer' (1963).

81 'Chaos' in T. Honderich, *The Oxford Companion to Philosophy* (Oxford, 1995) 129.

82 E. Lorenz, *The Essence of Chaos* (Washington, 1993) 3–4.

83 J. Jeans, *The Mysterious Universe*, 24.

84 Ibid. 3.

85 R. Stanard, *Science and Wonders*, 14.

86 Jeans, 3. S. Hawking, *A Brief History of Time.*

87 War-time codes based on apparently random sequences of numbers were broken, because of the existence of order within them.

88 S. Hawking, *A Brief History of Time*, 46.

89 Jeans, 109.

90 Teilhard de Chardin, *Hymn of the Universe*, n. 70.

91 Hawking, 125.

92 Cardinal Ratzinger. Address at Cambridge, reported in The Tablet 30 January 1988.

93 'Experientia docet' Horace, *Odes*.

94 M. Read, *Education and Cultural Tradition*, 14.

95 J. Sacks, *The Politics of Hope*, xvi.

96 E. Gilson, *The Unity of Philosophical Experience*, 237–8.

97 'For I do not do the good I want, but the evil I do not want is what I do.' Romans 7:19.

98 'There is in each one of us a spark of the divine essence that shines upon the very apex of what we call intellect, and makes us partakers of the Divine light', E. Gilson, *The Unity of Philosophical Experience*, 111.

99 A. Bloom, *The Closing of the American Mind* (1987).

100 Pope Paul VI, *Octogesima Adveniens* (Rome, 1971) Sec. 13.

101 D. Carr, *Educating the Virtues*, 256.

102 Report of the Advisory Council on Secondary Education.

103 S. S.Laurie.

104 'Medicine is an *ars cooperativa naturae*, an art of ministering, an art subservient to nature. And so is education.' J. Maritain, *Education at the Crossroads* (Yale, 1943) 30.

105 J. Sacks, *The Politics of Hope*, 63.

106 Boys' Brigades, Scouts and Guides, juvenile football clubs, arthletic clubs, dramatic societies, Church guilds have all but disappeared.

107 M. Mackintosh, *Education in Scotland Yesterday and Today.*

108 Sacred Congregation for Catholic Education, *The Catholic School*, v. 43.

109 M. Warnock, *A Common Policy for Education*, 118.

110 P. Hadot, *Philosophy as a Way of Life*, 275.

111 Report of Advisory Council on Secondary Education, Sections 48, 50, 90,

112 C. Dawson, *Enquiries*, 272.

113 J. Maritain, *Education at the Crossroads* (1943).

114 E. Gilson, *The Terrors of the Year Two Thousand* (Toronto, 1984 [1949]) reissued to celebrate the centenary of author's birth.

115 A. Huxley, *The Perennial Philosophy*, 5.

116 Pope John Paul II, *Crossing the Threshold of Hope*, 228.

117 G. Daly, *Creation and Redemption* (Dublin, 1988) 78.

Appendix One

The Christian Tradition in Scottish Education

The Lord's Prayer, the Christian teacher's charter, points to the dichotomy between spirit and matter which is at the heart of humanity's inbuilt tensions. Christian educators have to bear witness to two disparate aspects of reality, concern for this world and contemplation of the next, and strive to achieve a balance between them. Historically the balance has not always been achieved, and emphasis on one can result in neglect of the other.

For the first millenium after the birth of Christ, Christian education focused on the entry of God into the world, and its redemption through the life and death of Jesus. In the light of this overwhelming event, the paramount need of educators was to preserve and pass on the Good News. The injunctions, 'Seek ye first the Kingdom of God', and 'Render to Caesar the things that are Caesar's, and to God the things that are God's', set out their agenda.

As the Roman Empire declined, a monastic way of life, vital to the future educational process, emerged in the Egyptian desert,[1] and reached Scotland by the fourth or fifth century. An extraordinary flowering of spirituality ensued.[2] The Irish Sea was then at the centre of Celtic culture, and Ninian's *Candida Casa* was at the centre of the Celtic world. Whithorn became a training ground for Irish monks.[3] When Columcille laid the foundation of Scottish learning and education at Iona in the sixth century, the system in which he had been educated was more than a hundred years old.

In the sixth century of the Christian Era another monastic tradition, inspired by Benedict, took root in Italy.[4] In 597 AD, the year of Columcille's death, a Benedictine monk, Augustine (of Canterbury), was sent to England by Pope Gregory the Great, himself a Benedictine, with the mission of restoring the Christian life of the country. When, two centuries later, Charlemagne (742–814) forcibly reunited the territories of the fragmented Roman Empire, he set up an educational system designed to protect the Christian faith and preserve peace, and relied on the Benedictine Order to help achieve his objective. Schools to teach reading, singing, computation and grammar were to be provided in every monastery and cathedral, and all had to follow the Rule of Saint Benedict. The order became the great civiliser of Europe, and the Rule formed the basis of education for centuries afterwards.

In a world that had experienced barbarian invasions and the collapse of a great civil power, the desire for peace and stability was dominant, and the route to achieving them was seen to be through the spread of the Gospel. What was worth knowing and doing was that which was conducive to the knowledge and service of God. In western Christendom the spirituality that emerged was predominantly theocentric, and study of the natural order was neglected.

In the east a different outlook prevailed. Jewish, Islamic and Christian scholars had long been engaged in translating the works of Greek philosophy, science and literature into Arabic and Latin. This knowledge penetrated to the cities of the Mediterranean, and by the eleventh century nearly all the Greek texts that were to become known were available in the west. A major spiritual and cultural shift took place, one consequence of which was that the natural world began to be studied for its own sake.[5] Monastic and cathedral schools sprang up throughout the continent, their curriculum based on the new learning. From them the first European universities developed. The domination of the Catholic Church promoted a spiritual commonwealth in which a common language made communication between regions possible.

Towards the end of the first millenium monasticism in Scotland declined. Revival began about 1090 when Queen Margaret brought three Benedictine monks from Canterbury to found a Priory at Dumfermline. It continued in the reign of her son King David. By the middle of the twelfth century the Church in Scotland was organised in ten dioceses, a network of parishes was taking shape, and schools had begun to appear alongside the monasteries and cathedrals.

The emergence of the mendicant orders early in the thirteenth century marked a departure from the monastic tradition.[6] By the end of the century there were twelve Dominican and six Franciscan houses in Scotland. The curriculum of the schools began to expand, to include the secular arts and sciences. Grammar schools in Aberdeen, Edinburgh, Saint Andrews and Ayr stood in the grounds of Dominican foundations, and the first Congregation of Glasgow University was held in the Chapter House of the Black Friars. A trickle of Scots scholars to Oxford or Cambridge began, followed in the fourteenth century by a trend to Paris, Louvain, Orléans or Cologne rather than to England. From about 1380 onwards there was a sharp increase in the number of cathedrals and collegiate churches, and in 1411 the first Scottish university was founded at St Andrews.

A new, purely human culture was striving to come to light, associated with the advance of science, an activity based on measurement and observation of the physical world. The theocentric spirituality of the first millenium moved towards an anthropocentric mode, that echoed the Protagorean dictum 'Man is the measure of all things'. The balance shifted from contemplation of a spiritual universe to a search for understanding and mastery of the material world.

Humanism was accompanied by an evangelical revival directed towards purifying the Church. This Christian humanism was the inspiration of the Brothers of the Common Life, a religious order dedicated to the work of education.[7] Their system of instruction foreshadowed the *Ratio Studiorum* of the Society of Jesus, and had considerable influence on the development of Protestant education. Erasmus (1466–1534), the leading Christian humanist, and Johann Sturm (1507–1589), the founder of Protestant education, were educated by the Brothers, and Ignatius Loyola, founder of the Society of Jesus, and John Calvin, both came under their influence at the Collège de Montaigue in Paris, one of their institutions.

In 1543 Copernicus (1473–1543) published his great work *De Revolutionibus*, which put the sun at the centre of the cosmos, and led to wider understanding of a solar system simpler than the Ptolemaic. Scientific methodology penetrated European culture, and concentration on study of the natural world increased. Humanist education gained in strength particularly during the sixteenth century, which was to do more for the advancement of science than the fifteen centuries immediately preceding it. The Protestant Reformation was well under way, and the centuries-old unity of European Christendom was also being threatened by the rise of nation states in France, Spain and England.

When the Council of Trent was called in 1545, a counter-Reformation movement had already found expression through new religious orders whose concern was primarily with Christian education.[8] While the Council was in progress the *Book of Discipline* was published, in 1560. In 1563 the Thirty-Nine Articles were promulgated and the first wars of religion erupted in France. Half of Europe followed the teachings of Luther and Calvin; the other, which was also reformist, retained allegiance to the Papacy and to conservative theology. In Scotland, General Councils of the Catholic Church sketched out a programme of reform, which nevertheless failed. 'The problem in Scotland ... is not why reform came, but why it followed a Protestant and not a Catholic model.'[9]

When the Confession of Faith was accepted by the Scottish Parliament in 1560, Scotland was transformed at a stroke from a Catholic to a Protestant nation, in defiance of the reigning sovereign, and the thousand-year-old structure of the Catholic Church in Scotland collapsed. The effect was felt keenly in the area of schooling. The preexisting educational system was re-shaped by the *First Book of Discipline*, which enshrined a vision of a Godly Commonwealth based on Calvin's *Genevan Ordinances* and advocated a system that would cater for every stage from elementary school to university. Parish and burgh schools and the three universities would form a structure established by law, supported by public funds and supervised by authorities of Church and State. Religious education and the elements of literacy would come within reach of all; poverty would be no barrier to talent, and the school would be a place where all social classes would rub shoulders together. In the upshot the Kirk never obtained the money to realise its programme, and the Book remained largely a declaration of intent for more than a hundred years.

The Catholic Church in Scotland went into decline, sustained by a few missionary priests from Ireland and Europe and by a trickle of secular priests from Scots Colleges abroad.

Boys training for the priesthood had to be smuggled to these colleges. By the middle of the seventeenth century there were signs of renewal. In 1653 William Ballantine, ordained priest in Rome, was appointed Prefect Apostolic of non-Gaelic-speaking Scotland, and about 1663 a school under Ewen McAllister with sixty pupils opened in Skye.[10]

With the collapse of the Stuart dynasty in 1690 the Catholic Church was again in disarray. In 1694 Thomas Nicolson was consecrated Bishop, and appointed Vicar Apostolic for the whole of Scotland.[11] He took control of all the work of the mission, established a seminary at Preshome in Banffshire and ensured uniformity of doctrinal teaching.

During the seventeenth century, when Scotland was riven by religious strife, new movements in philosophy and science were emerging in Europe and England, driven by the work of Kepler, Galileo, Descartes, Pascal, Boyle, Newton, Halley and others. Most of these fathers of modern science displayed in their personal lives a search for a cosmological framework that would yet provide a place for the spiritual aspect of reality. For the scientists of this new age, it was one thing to reject the Ptolomaic view which had room for both God and Man, but another to find a replacement, consonant with the new science yet able to keep a place for the Godhead.

In Scotland, following on the Education Act of 1696 passed by an independent Scottish Parliament, an educational system founded on the principles of the *Book of Discipline* came into being. It was fostered after the Union of 1707 by a partnership between the Church of Scotland and the State which lasted into the twentieth century. The provision of elementary education, and the accessibility of secondary and university education maximised the talents of the country. Moral and religious teaching was a crucial part of the system. The Kirk sessions carried out inspections, and examined children in catechism. The Bible was part of every child's reading, and the system was beneficial to social order because the masters took such pains to instil basic Christian morality.

However, the Church of Scotland did not remain a united body, and an element of pluralism crept into Presbyterianism. When the universities of Glasgow and Edinburgh became the crucibles of the Scottish Enlightenment, schoolmasters began to give up practices in education on which earlier generations had laid great emphasis, such as ensuring that every child went to Church on Sunday so that lessons on Monday could begin with a close examination of the content and meaning of the sermon.

Roman Catholics and Episcopalians did not share in the cultural advance. Under the penal laws the establishment of a Catholic educational system was impossible. Priority was given to the education of boys for the priesthood, and attempts were made to set up small junior seminaries in remote places aiming to prepare students for the colleges abroad.[12]

During the latter half of the eighteenth century the Scots Colleges abroad faced enormous difficulties. Douai, closed in 1764, opened again in 1773 only to be closed a second time by the French revolutionary government in 1794. It was a time of Highland clearances and of emigration to new lands, and the Scottish Catholic population substantially decreased. In the last decade of the century Europe was in turmoil. In 1795 John Farquharson, Principal at Douai, opened a small chapel near the Gallowgate in Glasgow. This was later used as a school and became the first growth point of the post-Reformation Catholic parochial schools system.[13]

The spiritual mood of Scotland in the early nineteenth century was a fusion of the religious attitudes of the Reformation with the rationalism of the French Revolution. Although the educational system still operated on a religious base, the shift to an anthropocentric mode became more pronounced. 'The Church of Scotland no longer sought to force its own view of ecclesiastical polity on every citizen, nor to direct all social effort to the single end of building the City of God upon earth.'[14] The Scottish Enlightenment embodied faith in man's ability to determine his own destiny along with faith in the appeal to reason and to law, attitudes not confined to the intelligentsia, but accepted also in the artisan class who were also children of the Enlightenment, and who hoped that social inequality could and would be ended by moral pressure and by reason.[15] The democratic culture which these attitudes engendered was reinforced by a strong and independent religious tradition accepted at every level of society. 'The social authorities supported the wide diffusion of education, and endorsed an ethic of individual achievement.'[16]

At university level the educational ethos emphasised philosophy and intellectual achievement, and this was handed on to the clergy and teachers. The integration of religious belief and daily experience that had been fostered by the parochial schools began to be eroded by an educational ideal in which the pursuit of philosophical coherence, a product of human reason, gradually replaced devotion to divinely-revealed truth. In effect, the educational aim that had been derived from the teaching of Saint Augustine, was replaced by one drawn from the thinking of Pelagius, his redoubtable adversary.

When in the nineteenth century the rate of social change accelerated in an increasingly industrialised and urbanised society, the parochial schools were overwhelmed. The Church of Scotland moved into the field of urban education, opening sessional schools supported by individual congregations. As industrial and commercial activity increased, the urban middle class began to push for change in education, and the burgh schools became the focus of pressure directed mainly towards improvement at secondary level.

By the time of the Reform Act of 1829 the Catholic community in Scotland had grown to around 70,000, and Catholic schools became a necessity. In 1817 a Catholic Schools Society was formed in Glasgow. A small band of native Scottish priests made strenuous efforts to open schools, among them John Davidson and John Gordon in Greenock, William Thomson and Thomas Wallace in Ayrshire, and John Murdoch (later Bishop) in Pollokshaws in 1829. Especially influential in this development were parish priests Peter Forbes and Archibald Chisholm, who were instrumental in bringing two French Religious teaching Orders, the Marist Brothers and the Franciscan Sisters, to Glasgow.[17]

Attempts by the voluntary agencies to provide education attracted Government interest, and gave rise to the introduction of grants-in-aid of education. In 1839 the pupil-teacher system was instituted throughout the United Kingdom, and teacher-training colleges were established.

Division within the Kirk, exacerbated by state interference in church government, came to a head in the Disruption of 1843, when a third of the ministers left to form the Free Church. 'The Disruption ... was the most spectacular ecclesiastical event in modern Scotland. It created a large and influential denomination almost literally overnight.'[18] Thereafter there was a hope that the universities would assume responsibility for the nation's spiritual leadership, and achieve the practical reaffirmation of the moral ideals of Scottish life. However, from the 1830s they had come more and more under the control of the state, which provided much of their finance.[19] The requirement that lay professors should declare allegiance to the Church of Scotland by subscribing to the Confession of Faith was abolished. The Presbyterian churches retained their influence in education by controlling the teacher-training colleges, but in effect the preservation of the Christian tradition in Scottish education came to rest more and more on the commitment of individual teachers, and on the separate efforts of all the Christian churches, whose relationships with the civil authorities followed divergent paths.

The Disruption had dealt a fatal blow to the ideal of the parochial community grouped around the Church. In 1861 the system of examination of teachers by the Presbytery was abolished, and replaced by a process of monitoring by a University Board. Schoolmasters were no longer required to sign the Confession of Faith, though they still had to undertake to uphold the authority of Scripture. The religious basis of the national system was being revised, while simultaneously the tiny Catholic sector was growing in strength through the work of Religious teaching Orders, whose efforts were buttressed by the denominational inspectorate, vital to the development of the embryonic Catholic system.[20]

The religious climate was changing. By the 1860s a scientific and philosophical revolution, exemplified by the work of Hegel, Marx, Engels, Darwin, Huxley and others, was shaking the foundations of Christian belief. In 1859 *On the Origin of Species* was published. Powerful voices, Huxley's and Arnold's among them, called for changes in the school curriculum, particularly in the areas of science and physical geography, even at the elementary stage.[21] The secularisation of western civilisation was increased by scientific and technological advances which added to the prosperity and materialism of the major industrial nations. In the struggles beween Church and State, civil authorities were in the ascendent and the Catholic Church entered a period of withdrawal from the world.

The Education (Scotland) Act of 1872, which set up the Scotch (later Scottish) Education Department, ushered in the modern age of Scottish education. Thereafter responsibility lay with the State. Religious education was tolerated but not fostered. Episcopalians and Roman Catholics chose not to enter the public system because of their determination to strive for what they saw as the essential interdependence of religion and education. In many respects they were working towards the traditional aim of the Presbyterian churches, 'that religion should inform the whole of education'.[22]

Once a national system of primary education had been established, the Department set about reforming the secondary sector. A Leaving Certificate was instituted that set standards for university entrance, and provided an objective for girls hitherto debarred from higher education. In 1892 women were admitted to the universities.

During Queen Victoria's long reign religion remained an important force in Scottish politics. The bourgeoisie shared with the mass of the people an ideology based on free enterprise and on the traditional virtues of respectability and self-help.

By the end of the reign social cohesion was wearing thin. In response to the demands of the increasingly affluent middle class, a form of secondary education emerged that would provide for social and material advancement and preparation for entry into the professions. It offered continuity from primary through secondary to the university stage, and, as a corollary, a tight selection process at the crucial points of entry.

1872 was a parting of the ways among those who sought to preserve the Christian ethos of Scottish education. Thereafter the gap between the State and the voluntary sectors widened. The targets set by the Scottish Education Department were well beyond the capacity of the nascent Catholic sector, whose first priority had to be the provision of primary schools, adequately staffed by properly qualified teachers, before it could hope to expand at the secondary level. In 1894 a Training College for women, which opened at Dowanhill in Glasgow under the direction of the Sisters of Notre Dame de Namur, was a major step in this direction. Progress was slow, and if several Religious teaching Orders had not borne the burden of Catholic secondary education at this time the Catholic sector could not have survived.

BETWEEN THE WARS

The Education (Scotland) Act of 1918 continued the work begun in 1872. It extended to the secondary sector the concepts that had informed the approach to primary education. It adhered to the ideal of education for all and preservation of continuity from the primary to the university stage, and made financial arrangements that would make that continuity a reality for a greatly expanded spectrum of the population. It enshrined a concept of secondary education for all 'who were fit to profit from it'. Post-primary education would be provided at differing levels suited to the capacities of pupils, in secondary schools graded Junior or Senior. Authority was wielded by Ad Hoc Committees elected by Proportional Representation.

The Act aimed at developing an educated community marked by religious toleration and equal opportunity for all. It made possible the evolution of a system of denominational education under State control, supported by public funds. Existing Catholic schools transferred into the control of the new Ad Hoc authorities, and a distinctive Scottish dual system came into being.

Under the Act the denominational sector had to meet the legal requirements, and also satisfy the ecclesiastical authorities in respect of a greatly expanded commitment to religious education, now to be provided at a higher level and to a wider spectrum of the population than before. In spite of manifold difficulties, the Catholic sector flourished. There was an immediate upsurge in the demand for secondary places, and an improvement in the vital area of supply of teachers. The number of Catholic university graduates multiplied. A new degree of social mobility was experienced, and the conviction grew that the Catholic educational tradition had a distinctive contribution to make to the cultural and social life of society at large.

The experience of the non-denominational sector was rather different. Efforts to make religious instruction mandatory in the public schools had not succeeded, and the Church of Scotland had to be content with securing that the 'use and wont' provision, contained in the Preamble to the Act of 1872, was expressly affirmed in the main body of the 1918 Act. The danger was seen to lie in the difficulty of religious teaching, its lack of definition and its ineffectiveness, especially for older pupils.[23]

Scotland was still formally a religious country. By 1930 the Catholic Church claimed around eleven per cent and the Church of Scotland about twenty-six per cent of the population as adherents. Nevertheless the Kirk was in a state of decline which was expected to continue.[24]

The Thirties was a time of stress in economic, political and cultural life. There was never less than fourteen per cent of the insured labour force out of work, and in the West Central belt unemployment averaged twenty-five per cent.[25] World trade collapsed, and with it went what was left of the prosperity of the Clyde Docks and shipbuilding industry. Because of financial stringency, many praiseworthy schemes of the 1918 Act did not come into effect. The proposed raising of the school leaving age to fifteen did not happen until after World War II; the proposal for compulsory further education was also a casualty, and free secondary education did not come about until 1945.

The relationship of the churches to civil authority was redefined by the Local Government (Scotland) Act 1929, which placed responsibility for education on local authority committees on which the churches were represented.

The Act also decreed that no Council could discontinue religious instruction without first obtaining majority approval in a poll of local government electors. Although the Christian tradition of the schools seemed to be protected by these enactments, the dichotomy between religious and secular education that had been introduced in 1872 remained, and increasingly ensured the priority of the secular aspect in the educational process.

The response of the Church of Scotland to these developments is outlined in its *Church, School and Chaplain Report* in 1987: 'Out of the 1918 situation there emerged the Scottish Joint Committee on Religious Education … [which aimed] to foster religious education by preparing and publishing syllabuses and teaching aids.… Its materials had no statutory authority'. The most serious weakness was to confuse educational with evangelical aims.

> For long the SJC was frankly evangelical in its aims … to ensure understanding of the great affirmation of the Christian faith as revealed in the Bible, to relate the personal and community life of the children to Christian moral standards and to train them in habits of worship so far as it falls within the province of school life... so that ultimately the child may be brought to believe in the Lord Jesus Christ.[26]

The partnership in education of the established Church and the civil authority in an increasingly secularised society could not continue indefinitely on such a basis. This was in contrast to the experience of the Catholic sector, which in 1918 entered a new phase from which the community was to benefit in many ways. Nevertheless the Church's control over its schools diminished. Parish priests were no longer the managers of the primary schools, and their position vis-à-vis the secondary sector was even less clear. Curriculum priorities were set by the State, and formal religious education no longer stood firmly at the centre of the educational process. The position of the Religious teaching Orders weakened, and the preservation of the Christian ethos of the schools became ever more dependent on the commitment of the lay men and women who staffed the growing number of Catholic schools.

The Church provided training for Catholic teachers, supplementing that required by law. All were expected to share in the work of religious instruction, and the Church's approval was a recognition not only of suitability to hold moral authority over children, but also of satisfactory completion of a course of training in Religious Education. The system recognised the central role of Religious Education in the formation of the young, while helping to maintain in students a consciousness of the importance of the role of the teacher.

By 1939 a distinctive Catholic school system had emerged. The primary schools retained their strong religious character, and formed the base for an expanded secondary sector in which Religious teaching Orders still exerted considerable influence. Teachers accepted that a fundamental aim of education was the spiritual formation of the child.[27]

> To be worthy of the name, education must be directed to the development of the moral character of the the child more than to the development of its intellectual faculties. 'Manners makyth Man', and the Catholic Church knows no other means of moral development than the Christian religion with its motives, its sanctions and its practices.[28]

The State secondary schools were based on an efficient primary system, demanded a high standard of entry monitored by the Qualifying Examination, and maintained a clear distinction between junior and senior secondary levels of work. They recognised to a limited extent the need for religious education, but saw it as the responsibility of the parents and the Church rather than the school, whose priority was seen to be for intellectual training. The Catholic schools took on something of the aspect of their state contemporaries, but in the matter of religious education preserved a distinctive character. Religious teaching was not inspected by the Scottish Education Department, and had no place in the Leaving Certificate.

By the 1930s, Religious Instruction was allowed two periods per week in every Protestant school, but much of the teaching was superficial and unenthusiastic. The situation in RC schools was different: spiritual matters were the reason for their existence.[29]

Towards the end of the brief interlude between the two great wars a revised Day Schools (Scotland) Code redefined secondary education in terms of the pupil's development rather than the demands of the curriculum. Its implementation was prevented by the outbreak of the Second World War.

AFTER WORLD WAR II

For all of Europe from the Atlantic to the Urals the fratricidal conflict of 1939–45 left a legacy of material damage and human suffering on an unimaginable scale. In Britain the people had to endure conditions of austerity in some ways more stringent than in wartime. Young men were still being called up for national service. Consumer goods of all kinds were severely rationed, and a black market flourished. The severe winter of 1946–47 brought added hardships; yet the restoration of the fabric of the European nations began, spurred by the frenetic activity of the people and fuelled by financial and material aid from the United States of America.

A new world was struggling to be born. The western nations, conscious of the horrors of the Shoah and hypnotised by the threat of nuclear war, were subjected to political and social upheavals that brought convulsive changes in economic life. The League of Nations gave place to the United Nations Organisation; France and Germany began a co-operation that led to the formation of the European Community; the British and Communist Empires began to disintegrate; independent nations emerged in Africa and Asia; new philosophical movements swept through Europe and America, and the drain away from the mainstream Christian churches quickened. In Britain the Welfare State was born

The years of austerity passed, and the world economy entered a phase of prosperity in which the United Kingdom shared. Standards of living rose. The dependence on female labour of a nation at war continued in peacetime, and women were able more and more to take up gainful employment outwith the home. The Second Vatican Council revolutionised the concept of the structure of the Catholic Church, initiated a new era of ecumenism, and laid guidelines aimed at ending the poison of anti-Semitism.

With increasing affluence a new society, dubbed permissive, emerged, marked by uncertainty about standards rather than by any positive understanding of what could or could not be permitted. Communication between the generations became more than ordinarily difficult. Spectacularly, the concept of the family as the fundamental unit of society was eroded by sexual libertarianism and emphasis on an ill-defined notion of egalitarianism. The consequences of the breakdown in traditional values became apparent in widespread vandalism, broken homes, divorces, child abuse, abortions, drug addiction, crime, alcoholism and mental illness. Problems of the Welfare State were exacerbated by the advent of large numbers of commonwealth citizens drawn in to meet the demand for labour in those menial but necessary tasks that the increasingly affluent indigenous population disdained to undertake. With a simultaneous decline in formal church membership and in institutional religion generally, the power of the churches to maintain meaningful contact with the rising generations and with the most disturbed sectors of the community substantially decreased.

The industrial malaise which had long afflicted the south-west of Scotland was reasserted, and its heavy industries went into terminal decline. Technological change stimulated development in a bewildering range of activities, sounding the death knell of the age of iron and steam. Electricity, gas and oil ousted coal; and what had survived of the textiles industries gave way to proliferating man-made fibres. Automated devices replaced a human workforce, and new industrial competitors emerged in other parts of the world. A continuing high rate of emigration concealed the underlying situation.

The country as a whole faced an acute housing shortage. The New Towns Act designated East Kilbride in 1947 and Cumbernauld in 1956, the latter specifically to take overspill from Glasgow. Livingstone and Irvine followed in 1962 and 1966 respectively. Glasgow produced plans for one of the most ambitious slum clearance schemes in Europe, phased over twenty-five years, which aimed at overspilling large sections of its population into new towns, or into such older settlements as could be persuaded by financial or other considerations to accept them. The breakdown of old, established communities that followed was a significant cause of the difficulties facing the educational system.

Within this extraordinary scenario the Scottish educational system set about renewing itself. The Education Act of 1945 had pointed to a new type of schooling designed to suit the many as well as the old had fitted the few. The school leaving age was to be raised to fifteen and later to sixteen years; adequate and efficient provision of free primary, secondary and further education was to be made; Junior Colleges were to be set up for the compulsory part-time education of young persons of fifteen to eighteen; milk and meals were to be provided in all schools; and marriage would no longer be a bar to the employment of women teachers. Primary and secondary education were redefined in relation to the age, aptitude and ability of pupils, rather than in curricular or structural terms. Education authorities were required to devise schemes for promoting pupils from the primary to the secondary stage, and to ascertain the kind of courses from which each pupil would be likely to benefit.

A far-reaching and often agonising revolution took place, in which accepted functions and objectives were subject to a fierce reappraisal, which recognised the natural right of all children to receive an education allowing them to develop to their fullest potential, and that

> a liberal state ... will ensure through education that the creative energies of a new generation are used to direct the forces of change along lines that are socially desirable and in general accord with the nation's traditions and practices.[30]

The result was the emergence of the comprehensive secondary schools system. Selection procedures for the transfer of pupils from the primary to the secondary stage were abolished; the curriculum expanded the better to meet the needs of individual pupils, and the pastoral role of the school in the matter of social education was extended. The philosophical shift enshrined in the Education Act demanded revision both in the content of the curriculum and in the methods used to impart it, and the emergence of ultra-large comprehensive schools brought to light a range of pupil needs previously ignored or unsuspected. The content of every subject was scrutinised; new subjects were introduced and old re-written, and methods of organising the work of pupils fundamentally altered. The classical tradition went into decline, the approach to the teaching of language was seriously affected, and the opportunity for pupils to benefit from their heritage in the languages and literature of European civilisation was substantially reduced. An upheaval in the teaching of Mathematics was followed by the introduction of a wide range of scientific concepts needed to enable the pupil to move confidently into the changing world outside. An unparalleled revolution in communications transformed the educational scene, and weakened the position of the teacher as a main source of intellectual and moral nourishment for the young.

The calling of the Second Vatican Council was a matter of supreme importance for all concerned with education.[31]

> [Its documents] are especially noteworthy for their concern with the poor, for their insistence on the unity of the human family and therefore on the wrongness of discrimination, and for their repeated emphasis on the Christian's duty to build a just and peaceful world, in co-operation with all men of good will.[32]

Its *Decree on Ecumenism* had an immediate bearing on the cherished dream of Pope John XXIII, the reunion of all Christians. The thrust of the *Declaration on Christian Education* was insistence on the integration of Christian Education into human life in all its aspects.

> Christian Education is in the world and … for the world,… by contributing to the whole human community.… We note the strong emphasis on the intellectual values of all education and an appeal for all to strive to achieve the highest development of the human mind … this must be done in the framework of the moral formation of man and in the fullness of his supernatural destiny.[33]

At the time of the Council Scottish education had entered a critical phase. Too rapid expansion led to a serious shortage of teachers. The turbulence evident in the educational community reflected a deep-seated spiritual malaise in society at large. A loss of moral certainty in the adult population, experienced nationwide, resulted in the erosion of parental authority, confusion in the minds of the young and decline in respect for authority generally. The civil authority reacted by introducing a structure of personal, vocational and curricular guidance in all secondary schools.[34] In parallel with this development the Catholic Education Commission, instituted in 1972 to advise the Catholic Hierarchy on educational matters, set about introducing equally radical remedies.

GUIDANCE

A paradigm shift in the concept of the roles of the school and the teacher took place. Pastoral aspects of the teacher's work increased, and specialist qualifications in Guidance were introduced. In 1974 a Teaching Qualification in Religious Education for Secondary Education was introduced and Specialist Teachers of Religious Education began to be trained. Section 66(2) of the Education (Scotland) Act 1980, which forbade inspection of Religious Instruction by H. M. Inspectors, was repealed by the Education (Scotland) Act 1981, and in 1983 inspection of Religious Education by H. M. Inspectorate began.

In the last decades of the twentieth century there was no reduction in the rate of sociological change. Regionalisation came and went. Reduction of the schools population, a consequence of the use of abortion and other methods of artificial birth control, resulted in school closures and a decline in the number of teacher-training colleges and finally their absorption into the universities.

A fundamental question for educators, enunciated in the Report of the Advisory Council on Secondary Education in 1949, of 'how to pass on the moral and social inheritance' of the nation, has to be answered in the current post-modern ethical context. For one hundred and fifty years there was a creeping secularisation of the national system. Religious education was tolerated rather than encouraged, and secularisation has increased, principally, since 1945, through an unbalanced extension of the limits of freedom exercised by the young.

THE THIRD MILLENIUM

In the first decade of the twenty-first century the emphasis on secular aspects of education continues. Familiarity with spiritual reality fades, with a consequent dire misunderstanding of the human condition and of the true nature and destiny of mankind.

> Modern materialism ... is unbalanced and increasingly damaging in its long term consequences. Science has tried to assume a monopoly, even a tyranny, over our understanding. We are only now beginnng to gauge the disastrous results of this outlook.[35]

One of the distinctive features of the Scottish educational system since 1918 has been the co-existence within it of denominational and non-denominational sectors under central control. While there has been some convergence between these two sectors, the problems facing them are not identical. For the non-denominational sector, the central problem is to develop a moral code, independent of foundation in religious faith, but acceptable in a multicultural society. For the denominational system the problems are, how to fulfil simultaneously its religious and secular responsibilities, while instilling in its pupils a mindset integrating traditional religion and modern scientific knowledge. These are problems of a profoundly philosophical nature that should be at the centre of the thinking of the now expanded faculties of education in the Scottish universities.

In 1968 Notre Dame College expanded into a new building at Bearsden while retaining its original premises at Dowanhill. Craiglockhart expanded *in situ*. Degree-awarding powers were extended to Colleges of Education, and Notre Dame gained validation for its courses from the Council of National Academic Awards. National qualifications for Special Teachers of Religious Education were introduced, and agreement was reached between the Scottish Education Department and the Catholic Education Commission that H. M. Inspectors had a right to inspect professional aspects of religious education in Catholic schools.

In 1981 Notre Dame and Craiglockhart Colleges were closed, and St Andrew's College of Education was set up on the site at Bearsden as the National Catholic College of Scotland. Thereafter all prospective Catholic teachers were required to follow the course in Religious Education provided there. Distance Learning courses were introduced for students unable to attend there, backed by in-service courses at bases in Edinburgh and Dundee.

The approval of teachers to posts in Catholic schools in Scotland is the concern of the Hierarchy. In view of the many changes affecting Religious Education, the Commission approached the government to discuss an amendment to the Education (Scotland) Act 1980 reaffirming the right of the local bishop to 'approve as to religious belief and character' any teacher to be appointed to a Catholic school. This amendment became part of the Self-Governing Schools etc (Scotland) Act, 1989.

When the fall in student numbers reached the tertiary level, the organisation of higher education was again overhauled. The Council for National Academic Awards was wound up, and St Andrew's College became an Associate College of the University of Glasgow. This inherently unstable situation maintained until 1999, when the University's Department of Education, the Department of Adult and Continuing Education, the Teaching and Learning Service, the Centre for Science Education and St Andrew's College merged to form a ninth Faculty, the Faculty of Education, in which teacher education and the study of education would be provided in the context of a multidisciplinary research environment. It would continue to fulfil the existing role of St Andrew's College in initial teacher education for Catholic schools, guided by a Board of Catholic Education particularly concerned with the preparation of teachers for Catholic schools.

1 Athanasius, Bishop of Alexandria, the biographer of Saint Antony, carried the story of the Desert Fathers to Milan and Trier.

2 Martin of Tours (335–397), Augustine of Hippo (350–430) and Basil (329–379) founded monastic settlements within half a century of each other.

3 T. W. Moody and F. X., Martin, *The Course of Irish History*, 67. Enda, whose school on the Aran Islands formed many Irish abbots, was trained at Whithorn.

4 Benedict (480–583) founded Monte Cassino Abbey in 529, and wrote his Rule there.

5 A. C. Crombie, *Augustine to Galileo*, 6.

6 Both the Franciscans (Grey Friars) and Dominicans (Black Friars) were founded about 1216.

7 Founded in the Netherlands towards the end of the fourteenth century.

8 Among them were the Ursulines founded in 1535, and the Society of Jesus in 1540.

9 T. C. Smout, *A History of the Scottish People*, 56.

10 J. Darragh, *The Catholic Hierarchy of Scotland* (1986) 116.

11 Ibid. 123.

12 Ibid. 6 ff. Seminaries were established at Preshome in Banffshire in 1694, Loch Morar in 1714, Scalan in Banffshire 1716, Aquhorties, Aberdeenshire in 1799. Loch Morar, closed in 1715, refounded at Arisaig in 1737, disbanded after Culloden in 1746, refounded at Glenfinnan in 1767, disbanded again in 1779. Refounded in 1783, transferred to Lismore in 1803. In 1829 colleges at Aquhorties and Lismore were joined to become the national junior seminary at

Blairs in Aberdeenshire.

13 T. A. FitzPatrick, 'Catholic Education in Glasgow, Lanarkshire and South-West Scotland before 1872', *Innes Review*, 36/2 (1985) 86–96.

14 T. C. Smout, 482.

15 R. D.Anderson, *Education and Opportunity in Victorian Scotland*, 24.

16 T. C. Smout, 482.

17 T. A. FitzPatrick, 'Catholic Education in Glasgow, Lanarkshire and South-West Scotland before 1872', 86-96.

18 C. G. Brown, *Religion and Society in Scotland since 1707*, 25.

19 R. D. Anderson, 36. Appointment of about half of all chairs was made by the Crown.

20 The denominational inspectorate was ended in 1869 by the Revised Code.

21 T. A. FitzPatrick, *No Mean Service*, 43–48. When the first Roman Catholic teacher-training college in Scotland was opened at Dowanhill with the approval and support of the Scotch Education Department, a temporary science room had to be provided to meet the insistent demands of the Inspectorate for the teaching of science.

22 Church of Scotland Department of Education, *Church, School and Chaplain* (Edinburgh, 1987) 6.

23 Ibid. 6.

24 *Life and Work*, 14 July 1999.

25 S. G. Checkland, *The Upas Tree*, 35.

26 CSC 1987.

27 It was a common practice for Catholic teachers to attend the children's Mass on Sundays along with their pupils.

28 S. N. D., *Sister Mary of St Philip 1825-1905* (London, 1920).

29 J. Scotland, *A History of Scottish Education*, ii, 82.

30 Report of the Advisory Council on Secondary Education.

31 The Council opened on 11 October 1962 and closed on 8 December 1964.

32 Cardinal Shehan in the Introduction to W. J. Abbott SJ (ed.) *The Documents of Vatican II.*

33 G. E. Carter, Bishop of London Ontario. Commentary on 'The Declaration on Christian education' in W. J. Abbott SJ (ed.) *The Documents of Vatican II.*

34 *Guidance in Scottish Secondary Schools* (1968). *The Structure of Promoted Posts in Scottish Secondary Schools* (1971).

35 Prince Charles, *The Times*, 14 December 1996.

Appendix Two

Indoctrination and Freedom

All education is indoctrination

According to the Oxford Dictionary, the first definition of the word indoctrination is simply, to imbue with learning. That is, to teach or to instruct in a principle or subject.

When used in this sense, it can be said that all instruction is, or partakes of, the nature of indoctrination.

A further definition, however, is: to imbue with a doctrine, idea or opinion. This carries a different nuance, expressed more forcibly elsewhere, that indoctrination is 'teaching systematically a person or group of persons to accept a doctrine, especially uncritically'.[1] The thrust of this second definition is emphasised by the definition of a doctrine, as: a creed or body of teachings of a religious, political or philosophical group presented for acceptance or belief.

When used in this sense, indoctrination implies a purposefulness on the part of the teacher, which would not apply in circumstances where the pupil is left free to accept or reject the doctrine that is being presented.

The second definition conveys the pejorative sense in which the word is frequently used. It raises, without answering, a number of questions, which arise only when the subject matter being presented is open to doubt. The following are examples.

Does indoctrination in the pejorative sense depend on

the truth or falsity of the doctrine being presented? Does it depend on whether the teacher presenting it believes in it? Does indoctrination arise only when the doctrine presented is false, not proven or when taught by teachers who do not believe in it?

Consider the case of Ptolemy's vision of the universe. Was he guilty of indoctrination when he taught that the earth was at the centre of the universe? Were those who propagated his teaching also guilty? Is a teacher guilty of indoctrination when he propagates as true a doctrine which he knows not to be true?

In such a case, if the teacher maintains that the doctrine is true, knowing it is not, he is guilty of lying. If he teaches that the doctrine is not true, he is not guilty of indoctrination.

Can a system of education be said to be guilty of indoctrination when its teachers imbue their pupils with a doctrine which they believe to be true, but which is in fact false? This may have been the case for some teachers in Nazi Germany.

In such a case, does indoctrination depend on the extent to which the doctrine is accepted by the recipient? In this, or similar cases, the charge of indoctrination is brought by observers outside the system who are convinced not only that the doctrine in question is wrong, but that those presenting it must know that it is wrong. This implies that in issues of this nature there is a natural consensus about rightness and wrongness in human behaviour.

Does the guilt of indoctrination depend on the force or conviction with which a doctrine is presented, or on the extent to which its recipients are convinced of its truth? One contributer to the Millar Report attempted to rebut the charge (that teaching that the Bible is true is indoctrination) by claiming that the confusion and muddle about even the basic facts of the Bible in so many pupils gave the lie to the charge of indocrination. The confusion and muddle might mean merely that attempted indoctrination has failed.

How can an educational system avoid the charge of indoctrination in the pejorative sense? Should it restrict itself to teaching only doctrines that are known to be true, by teachers who believe them to be true, in a manner that leaves the pupil free to accept or reject them? Leaving aside the need to answer the question, What is Truth?, this is clearly not a practical proposition.

A system that upholds the primacy of the individual conscience is particularly vulnerable to the charge of indoctrination. Ideally, pupils should be brought to accept or reject propositions through intellectual conviction and willing assent. In the real world of the classroom they are expected to accept propositions on the authority of the teacher.

Pupils are not in a position to judge between one authority and another. In the case of the very young, that responsibility must rest with the parents. A point must arise when the authority of the parent should give way to the right of the child to make his or her own decisions. An educational system should take account of the need to prepare pupils for this critical point in their lives. There must therefore be a difference in approach to religious and moral education at the secondary and primary levels.

In its analysis of Education and Indoctrination, *A Good Life* bases its argument largely on the impact of value-judgments.[2] It acknowledges that the principle that 'religious or moral education must not indoctrinate' itself rests on value-judgments about man's existence and worth, which however are not usually made explicit. The introduction of the term value-judgment obscures the thrust of the argument, since it suggests that the weighing up of one belief or doctrine against others is the heart of the matter. If doctrines are to have value only relatively to each other, then it must follow that all teaching is indoctrination – some more, some less.

Against this, the Christian tradition holds that there is a bottom line of absolute truth which informs the values structure. It holds that God does exist, however much human accounts or mis-representations of the divine nature have obscured that reality, and that the truth for humanity has been revealed principally in the person of Jesus.

According to *The Tablet* of 3 February 2007 (page 13) the following statement appeared on the Downing Street website:

We, the undersigned petition the Prime Minister to make it illegal to indoctrinate or define children by religion before the age of 16; in order to encourage free thinking, children should not be subjected to any regular religious teaching or defined as belonging to a particular religious group according to the views of their parents or guardians.

The questions remain. What is doctrination? What is religion?

1 *Collins Concise Dictionary Plus* (1990).

2 *A Good Life*, 38.

Appendix Three
An Afterthought

Faith, Physics and Football

The waters saw you and trembled
The depths were moved with terror.

PSALM 76

In his colloquy to scientists at Castel Gondolfo, Pope John Paul II asked whether the time was ripe for a more nuanced interchange between religion and science. I would suggest that such an interchange could begin from a study of John D. Barrow's analysis of the limits of science as he put forward in his book *Impossibility.*

Consider the following: Euclid's geometry begins with the enunciation of axioms, that are statements on the truth of which there is general agreement. One of these is, that the shortest distance between two points is a straight line. From this there follows a description of a space of three dimensions, in which each dimension stretches to infinity.

This is essentially an abstract idea, which is useful as a basis for locating points in space. In this concept, points are located with reference to a fixed point, an origin from which distances may be measured in each dimension. It may then be assumed, and has been, that this abstract idea gives an accurate description of 'real' space, and that therefore real space is also of three dimensions that stretch to infinity in all directions.

This may or may not be so. To say that it is, is to make an assumption about the nature of space itself.

Other mental constructions are possible. For example, navigation or mapping on the surface of the earth can be carried out more accurately by spherical trigonometry than by plane trigonometry. In this case the co-ordinates (latitude, longitude) are curved, and points are located with reference to a fixed point at the centre of the earth. Such a construct is suitable for astronomy or spatial navigation. Should it therefore be assumed that this is what 'real' space is 'really' like?

A geometry using spherical, i.e. curved, co-ordinates is a non-Euclidean geometry. Such a geometry may fit real space better than Euclidean geometry does. According to E. T. Whittaker 'It is a matter of convenience, whether we prefer to have an easily intelligible geometry with complicated physical laws, or a less intelligible geometry with simple physical laws'.[1]

Now consider the following scenario and compare it with the biblical story of creation:

> Think of an old-fashioned football, consisting of an inner tube and an outer cover, inflated to become two enormous concentric spheres. As the football is inflated, the space between the skins increases.
>
> An ant situated on the surface of the inner tube could move in any direction. If it keeps moving long enough, it will eventually arrive back at it starting point. It inhabits a finite universe of two dimensions.
>
> A fly inhabiting the space between the inner and outer skins, moving parallel to the skins, would also eventually arrive back at its starting point, whatever direction it chose to go. To locate its position at any time on its journey of discovery, with reference to the space it inhabits, curved co-ordinates like latitude and longitude, would be suitable.

Suppose now that the football is inflated in such a way that the inner and outer skins recede from one another at a rate that increases as the football gets bigger. The fly now lives in an expanding universe. If its maximum speed of flight is less than the speed at which the skins are receding from it, it can never find out where the skins are. It is living in a space which is not infinite, and yet one whose limits it cannot know.

Now imagine the football to be inflated an unimaginable but real number of times, and let the fly increase and multiply. The space becomes very very large, but still limited. Instead of flies, think of galaxies, existing in an expanding non-Euclidean space. Instead of the fly's speed of flight we have the speed of light. If the rate of expansion exceeds the speed of light there will be no way of locating the limits of this space.

However this is not the whole story. There are other spaces, inside and outside the football, about which the fly can know nothing. Call the space outside Hyperspace, and the space inside the inner tube Hupospace, to distinguish them from the 'real' space which is the space the fly inhabits.[2]

Compare the above scenario with the Genesis story of creation.

Revised Standard Version

(1.2) The earth was without form and void, and darkness was upon the face of the deep, and the Spirit of God was moving over the face of the waters. [...] (1.6–7) And God said, Let there be a firmament in the middle of the waters and let it separate the waters from the waters. And God made the firmament and separated the waters which were under the firmament from the waters which were above the firmament.

Good News Bible

(1.2) The earth was formless and desolate, and the power of God was moving over the water. [...] (1.6–7) Let there be a dome to divide the water and keep it in two separate places.

Jerusalem Bible
(1.2) The earth was a formless void and there was darkness over the deep. [...] (1.6–7) God made the vault, and it divided the waters above the vault from the waters under the vault.

New English Bible
(1.2) The earth was without form and void made the vault, and separated the water under the vault from the water above it.

Knox Bible
(1.2) God, at the beginning of time created heaven and earth. Earth was still an empty waste, and darkness hung over the deep. [...] (1.6–7) Let a solid vault arise amid the waters, to keep these waters apart from those; a vault by which God would separate the waters which were beneath it from the waters above it.

Keeping in mind the inadequacy of language to describe the unknown, the consonance of the biblical and the scientific accounts of space is clear. The void, or the water, or the waters correspond to the situation that existed before the act of creation. It is Hyperspace, the 'space' outside the football, although the term 'space' as used here should be taken to mean 'the unknown'.

As a result of a singular act, the waters are separated by a firmament, dome or vault. The 'space' that appears within the dome or vault corresponds to the space between the skins of the football. The waters above the vault correspond to the space outside the football. Let us call this Hyperspace. The waters under the vault correspond to the space within the football. Let us call this Hupospace. The 'space' between the skins, which is 'curved', and expanding beyond limits that are knowable, is 'real' space. It is within this space that the universe accessible to human knowledge is created, and evolves.

This universe exists in a space whose limits cannot be

known, which is therefore in a sense infinite, but which is not infinite in an absolute sense because it is contained within a further, unknown and unknowable hyperspace.

To examine the difference between Hyperspace and 'real' space, imagine that the football is deflated unil it shrinks to vanishing point, to an infinitely small size, like a point in Euclidean space. Such a point is said to have no dimensions but can mark a location.

This description raises a difficulty. Is an infinitely small football the same thing as no football? Just as 'infinitely large' describes a quantity which exists and can increase but has no limit, so infinitely small means a quantity which exists and can decrease but has no known limit.

Is that limit No Thing?

In *Jehovah and Hyperspace*, Frank Parkinson describes this point as a singularity in Hyperspace having no dimensions. At this point (in his view) the Big Bang takes place, (the football begins to be inflated) and the cosmos begins to evolve.

The question remains, does Hyperspace exist? If so, are we to suppose that it exists in a Hyper-hyperspace? And so on *ad infinitum*?

In this scenario the cosmos, the 'created' universe, can be understood as being limited in time and space, and due to pass away in the fullness of time. Hyperspace will not.

1 E. T. Whittaker. *From Euclid to Eddington*, 36.
2 F. Parkinson, *Jehovah and Hyperspace* (2002).

Appendix Four

A Chronology

55 BC	Roman invasion of Britain.
	BIRTH OF CHRIST
23–79 AD	Life of Pliny. *Natural History* written.
70–80	Roman Fort at London. Eboracum (York) occupied by Romans.
c. 100–200	Christian schools in Alexandria.
	Christian Monasticism originates with Saint Anthony and the Desert Fathers in Egypt.
c. 120	*The Didache* (The Teaching of the Twelve Apostles).
122–127	Hadrian's wall constructed.
c. 142–143	Antonine's Wall constructed.
c. 160–220	Tertullian.
c. 185–254	Origen – value of secular learning.
c. 272–282	Birth of Constantine.
306	Constantine proclaimed Emperor at York.
313	Edict of Milan by Constantine and Licinius.
318–320	Donatist and Arian disputes. Donatists – a fanatical sect in North Africa. Arianism: 'Jesus differed in essence from the Father'.
	Council of Arles, attended by a bishop of York.
325	COUNCIL OF NICEA. The first Ecumenical Council; convoked by Constantine.
324–330	Constantinople founded.
327–328	Second Council of Nicea.
329	Birth of Saint Basil the Great, Father of Eastern Monasticism. His brother Saint Gregory of Nyssa and Saint John Chrysostom amalgamate pagan philosophy and Christian theology.
335	Birth of Saint Martin of Tours.

337	Death of Constantine the Great.
339	Saint Athanasius introduces Monasticism to Europe.
340	Birth of Saint Ambrose.
350	Birth of Saint Augustine of Hippo.
360	Birth of Saint Ninian.
	Saint Martin of Tours founds monastery at Ligugé.
	Saint Basil founds monastery at Pontus in Asia Minor.
c. 354	Birth of Pelagius.
372	Saint Martin consecrated Bishop of Tours.
379	Death of Saint Basil.
397	Deaths of Saints Martin and Ambrose.
415	Pelagius – accused of heresy before the Synod of Jerusalem. Thought that Free Will and teaching of the Law sufficient for salvation. Reaction against Gnosticism/Manichaeism/Fatalism.
430	Death of Saint Augustine.
c. 432	Death of Saint Ninian.
	Monastery and School of Sanctity at Whithorn.
	Saint Patrick in Ireland. Monastic way of life introduced to Ireland.
455	Sack of Rome by the Vandals.
c. 460	Death of Saint Patrick.
480–547	Saint Benedict, Father of Western Monasticism.
529	Saint Benedict founds Monte Cassino Abbey.
c. 540	Benedictine Rule written. Diocese of Glasgow founded by Saint Kentigern.
563	Saint Columba lands in Iona.
590	Saint Gregory the Great becomes Pope.
593	Saint Augustine of Cantebury arrives in Kent.
	Cathedral School founded at Chartres.
604	Death of Pope Saint Gregory.
673–735	The Venerable (Saint) Bede.
735–804	Alcuin of York, disciple of Bede.
890	Death of King Alfred the Great.
910	Monastery founded at Cluny.
1066	Norman Conquest.
1058–1093	Reign of King Malcolm III.
1070	Marriage of Malcolm and Saint Margaret.
	Benedictine Priory at Dumfermline.
1093	Death of Saint Margaret, Queen of Scotland.
1090–1153	Life of Saint Bernard of Clairvaux, founder of the Cistercian Order.
1100	School at Abernethy in Perthshire.

1120	Premonstratensian (Norbertine) Order founded.
	Premonstratensian Abbey at Whithorn.
	School at St Andrews.
	Completion of first stone Cathedral in Glasgow.
1124–1153	Reign of King David I.
1124	School at Dunfermline.
1128	Edinburgh receives its charter as a Burgh.
	Dunfermline Priory becomes an Abbey.
	School at Kelso.
1136	Melrose Abbey founded.
1142	Dundrennan Abbey founded.
1150	Jedburgh Abbey founded.
1160	School at Perth.
c. 1150	Origin of University of Paris.
c. 1170	Origin of Oxford University.
1174	Papal Bull establishes the Scottish Church.
1179	Third Lateran Council.
1180	School at Lanark.
1187	School at Linlithgow.
1192	Pope Alexander III declares the See of Glasgow *Filia Romanae Ecclesiae* (a Special Daughter of Rome).
1209	Order of Friars Minor founded by Saint Francis.
1215	Order of Preachers founded by Saint Dominic.
1225	Scottish Church given the right to hold independent Councils.
1200–1280	Life of Saint Albert (Albertus Magnus).
1214–1294	Life of Roger Bacon.
1225–1274	Life of Saint Thomas Aquinas.
1265–1308	Life of Blessed John Duns Scotus.
1313	Collège des Écossais founded in Paris.
1314	Battle of Bannockburn.
1320	Declaration of Arbroath.
c. 1350	Gerard Groote founds the Brothers of the Common Life.
1411	Foundation of Saint Andrews University.
1451	Foundation of Glasgow University.
1473	Birth of Copernicus.
1492	Voyage of Columbus to America. Jews and Muslims expelled fom Spain.
1495	Foundation of Aberdeen University.
1529	Saint Ignatius Loyola at Collège de Montaigue.
1535	Society of Jesus (Jesuits) and Ursuline Order founded.
1536	Johannes Sturm reorganises the educational system of Strasbourg.

1543	Death of Copernicus. Publication of *De Revolutionibus.*
1545	Council of Trent begins.
1560	Protestant Reformation in Scotland. *Book of Discipline.*
1562–1563	The First War of Religion in France.
1563	Council of Trent ends. Promulgation of the Thirty-Nine Articles.
1572	Saint Bartholomew's Day Massacre.
1576	Scots College founded at Douai.
1592	Birth of Comenius (Jan Amos Komensky).
1600	Scots College, Rome, re-founded.
1603	Union of Crowns of Scotland and England.
1612	Jesuits staff Scots College at Douai.
1615	Jesuits staff Scots College in Rome. Saint John Ogilvie martyred in Glasgow.
1620	First Irish Franciscan missionaries arrive in Scotland.
1625	Society of Saint Vincent de Paul founded.
1627	Scots College Madrid founded.
1637	Descartes: *Discours de la Méthode.* Episcopalian bishops driven from Scotland.
1638	National Covenant signed in Scotland.
1641	Comenius invited to England.
1650	Six Scottish priests meet in Paris, led by William Ballantine.
1651	Birth of Jean Baptiste de la Salle, founder of Frères des Écoles Chrétiennes, in Rheims.
1653	William Ballantine appointed first Prefect Apostolic of non-Gaelic Scotland.
1657	Comenius's *Magna Didacta* published in Amsterdam.
1663	Catholic School established on Skye by Ewen McAllister.
1670	Six free schools in France.
1675	Saint Jean Baptiste de la Salle founds two free schools for girls.
1682	Halley's Comet observed.
1684	Jean Baptiste de la Salle opens the first École Normale at Rheims.
1687	Newton's *Philosophiæ Naturalis Principia Mathematica* published.
1688	Halley's Meteorological Map. James II deposed.
1690	Locke's *An Essay Concerning Human Understanding.* Battle of the Boyne.

Presbyterianism established in Scotland.

1692 Massacre at Glencoe.

1694 Thomas Nicholson appointed Vicar Apostolic for the Catholic Church in Scotland.

1696 Act for Settling Schools passed by Scottish Parliament. Every parish to provide a schoolhouse and appoint a schoolmaster (no professional qualifications were required).

1697 Bishop Thomas Nicholson in residence at Preshome.

1698 Saint Jean Baptiste de la Salle opens École Normale in Paris.

1702 Accession of Queen Anne.

1707 Union of Parliaments of Scotland and England.

1708 John Wallace ordained priest at Preshome.

1714 Seminary founded at Loch Morar with seven boys.

Accession of George I.

1715 First Jacobite rebellion.

1716 Seminary re-opens at Scalan.

1718 Nicholson dies at Preshome. Succeeded by Bishop James Gordon.

1719 Publication of *Robinson Crusoe*.

Handel appointed Director of the Academy of Music.

1726 Famine in Ireland.

Gulliver's Travels published.

1727 Bishop Gordon Vicar Apostolic of the Lowland District.

Accession of George II.

1731 Hugh MacDonald, Vicar Apostolic of the Highland District.

1741 Irish famine ends.

Hume's *Essays Moral and Political* published.

1742 First performance of Handel's *Messiah*, in Dublin.

1744 Anson returns from voyage round the world.

1745 Second Jacobite rebellion.

1746 Massacre at Culloden. Death of Bishop James Gordon.

Alec Smith, Vicar Apostolic of the Lowland District.

1751 Birth of Saint Julie Billiart in Cuvilly, Picardy.

1752 Gregorian calendar adopted in the British Isles.

1759 Birth of Robert Burns.

1760 Accession of George III.

1760–1860 Highland Clearances.

1764 Society of Jesus suppressed in France by Louis XV.

College at Douai closed.

1767	Death of Alec Smith.
	James Grant appointed Vicar Apostolic of the Lowland District.
1773	College at Douai re-opens.
	Death of Hugh MacDonald.
	John MacDonald appointed Vicar Apostolic of the Highland District.
1775	American War of Independence.
1778	Catholic Relief Bill in England.
	Voltaire and Rousseau die.
	Fewer than 20 Catholics resident in Glasgow.
	Death of Bishop James Grant.
	George Hay appointed Vicar Apostolic of the Lowland District.
1779	Removal of restrictions on Irish trade.
	Saint Madeleine Sophie Barat born at Joigny, Burgundy.
	Death of John MacDonald. Succeeded by Alec MacDonald as Vicar Apostolic of the Northern District.
	John Geddes Coadjutor of the Lowland District.
1780	Anti-Catholic Gordon Riots in London. First Epsom Derby.
1788	New South Wales established as a penal colony.
1789	French Revolution: Church property seized, Religious Orders suppressed, schools closed.
1791	Death of Mozart.
	Boswell's *The Life of Samuel Johnson* published.
	Death of Alec MacDonald.
1792	French revolutionary government introduces the Civil Constitution of the Clergy.
	John Chisholm appointed Vicar Apostolic of the Northern District.
1793	Britain declares war on France.
1794	Society of Jesus founds college at Stonyhurst.
1795	Scots College at Douai closes for the second time.
	Principal John Farquharson opens a chapel in Glasgow near the Gallowgate.
1796	Death of Robert Burns.
1797	Experiment in Education: Bell's Monitorial System.
1798	Rebellion in Ireland suppressed.
1799	Death of John Geddes.
1800	Society of the Sacred Heart founded at Amiens by Saint Madeleine Sophie Barat for the education of girls of the upper classes, with free schools for the

poor where possible.
1801 Napoleon's Concordat with the Holy See.
1802 Treaty of Amiens. Temporary peace with France.
Edinburgh Review founded.
1803 Education Act for the better government of Parochial Schools in Scotland. Schoolmasters to be examined and approved by the Presbytery, and sign the Confession of Faith. Jurisdiction over all schoolmasters given to the Church of Scotland.
1804 Congregation of Notre Dame formed by Saint Julie Billiart.
Decree of Messidor June 1804: renewed threat to religious orders
1805 Battle of Trafalgar.
Alec Cameron appointed Vicar Apostolic of the Lowland District.
1807 Notre Dame Mother House moves to Namur.
1808 Parish of St Mirin, Paisley, founded.
1810 James Pillans introduces Lancaster's monitorial system to Edinburgh High School.
1811 Death of Bishop George Hay.
1812 In Edinburgh, Sunday Schools open in every Church of Scotland parish which later develop into Day Schools to teach reading.
1813 Parish of St Andrew, Dumfries, founded.
Pride and Prejudice published.
1814 Anglo-American War ends.
Waverley published.
St Peter's Catholic parish, Dalbeattie founded.
Death of John Chisholm.
Aeneas Chisholm appointed Vicar Apostolic of Highland District.
1815 Waterloo: Fall of Napoleon.
Creation of the Commission de l'Instruction Publique.
Primary education made compulsory in France.
1816 Foundation of St Andrew's parish, Glasgow, and St Mary's, Greenock.
Robert Owen institutes Infant Schools at New Lanark.
David Stow, influenced by Thomas Chalmers, Minister of the Tron Kirk, starts a Sabbath school in Glasgow.
Catholic schools functioning in Blantyre and Paisley.

Death of Saint Julie Billiart.

1817 École Normale d'Enseignement Mutuel set up by the Commission de l'Instruction Publique.

Marist Brothers founded by Saint Marcellin Champagnat.

Religious Congregations in France required to be authorised legally.

Catholic Schools Society formed in Glasgow.

1818 Two Catholic schools operating in Glasgow in Gallowgate and Gorbals.

Death of Aeneas Chisholm.

1819 Catholic school opens in Bridgeton.

1820 Accession of George IV.

In Belgium, every teacher conducting a class required to obtain a diploma of good conduct and teaching capacity.

Ronald MacDonald appointed Vicar Apostolic of the Highland District.

1822 Parish of Saint Margaret in Ayr founded.

Catholic school operating in Anderston, Glasgow.

1824 Glasgow Infants School Society founded.

1825 Five Catholic schools operating in Glasgow.

In Belgium, a further *Brévet de capacité* has to be re-earned in addition to the *Brévet* (required from 1805) by those who wish to teach.

Death of Alec Cameron.

Alec Paterson appointed Vicar Apostolic of Lowland District.

1826 Wood's Sessional School, Edinburgh, becomes a 'Model' school.

1827 Alec Paterson appointed Vicar Apostolic of the Eastern District, and Ronald MacDonald of the Western District.

1828 'Model' Infant School established in the Drygate by Glasgow Infant School Society. David Stow's training system begins. His educational philosophy intended to mould character by moral training based on Scripture. First demands for Chairs of Education in Scottish Universities, and for university involvement in the training of teachers.

1832 Death of Sir Walter Scott.

1843 Disruption in the Church of Scotland. Number of training colleges double. In Edinburgh almost all staff and students of the Sessional schools (Church

of Scotland) became Free Church members. Rector, staff and majority of students leave the established Church College. Stow leads a mass exodus from the Normal School at Dundas Vale.
The Redemptorists open a foundation at Falmouth in Cornwall.

1844 Population of Glasgow 200,000 (c. 45,000 Irish).
Catholic school in Burgher Row, near Partick Cross.

1845 Church of Scotland Training School opens in Johnson Terrace, Edinburgh.
Notre Dame Sisters go to Penryhn near Falmouth at the invitation of the Redemptorists. New convent and a Training College at Mount Pleasant, Liverpool.

1846 Pupil-Teacher system introduced throughout England and Scotland. Five-year apprenticeships in school. Exam at eighteen. Maintenance available at colleges through Queen's Scholarships.

1847 Franciscan Sisters and Sisters of Mercy open schools in Glasgow.
Town Council take over Glasgow's water supply.
Free Church Training College opens in Cowcaddens.
First Notre Dame School in England opens at Penrhyn with five or six poor children.

1858 Marist Brothers in Glasgow.
On the Origin of Species published.

1859 St Aloysius' College, Glasgow, founded.

1876 Chairs of Education at St Andrews and Edinburgh.

1878 Pope Leo XIII restores Scottish Hierarchy; Charles Eyre appointed first post-Reformation Archbishop of the restored See of Glasgow.
Kelvinside Academy opens.
Glasgow Academy reopens as a private venture at Kelvinbridge.
Govan School Board builds a school at Hillhead.

1879 Church of Scotland Training College, Chambers Street, Edinburgh.

1881 Visit of Cardinal Manning to Glasgow.

1883 Queen Margaret College acquired for the education of women.
Rev. J. A. Maguire (future Archbishop) in charge at St Peter's Partick.
School with five hundred pupils opens at Whiteinch.
Death of Karl Marx.

1889 Education Act reforming Universities. Student Representative Councils introduced.

1891 *Rerum Novarum* promulgated by Pope Leo XIII.

1892 Scottish Universities open to women. Some admitted to the Medical Faculty. Saint Peter's Seminary transferred from Partickhill to a new building built by Archbishop Eyre at New Kilpatrick.

1894 Sisters of Notre Dame de Namur invited by Archbishop Eyre to open a Teacher Training College.

Premises at Dowanhill obtained.

First Principal Sister Mary of Saint Wilfrid (Mary Adela Lescher).

First Catholic post-primary department in Lanarkshire opens at St Augustine's, Coatbridge.

1895 Scotch Code: Link of Teacher Training with Universities renewed by establishment of Local Committees.

St Andrews and Aberdeen begin training students for teaching.

Cardinal Vaughan removes the ban on attendance of Catholics at Universities.

First students enrolled at Dowanhill for teacher training.

1897 Notre Dame High School opens Junior Training Centre for Prospective Teachers.

1899 'Charlotte Street' (Our Lady and St Francis) Glasgow, becomes a Higher Grade School and a Junior Student Centre; also Elmwood.

Pope Leo XIII consecrates the human race to the Sacred Heart of Christ: 'All men are potentially members of Christ's body' (Saint Thomas Aquinas).

1900 University College Dundee begins training students for teaching.

1901 School Leaving Age raised to fourteen.

In France, Religious Congregations required by Law to be authorised by the State.

1902 Death of Archbishop Eyre.

1903 Supplementary classes introduced into some Primary Schools. Glasgow University to train students for teaching.

St Peter's Church, Partick, opens.

1905 Pupil-Teacher system modified.

In France all Catholic schools are closed. Church

property secularised.
Conversion of J. S. Phillimore.
Provincial Committees each connected to a University and responsible to Scotch Education Department replaces Local Committees. Catholic Education Council takes over work of Catholic Schools Committee.

1906 Church of Scotland Training College (Dundas Vale) and Free Church Training College (Stow College) transfer to the Glasgow Provincial Committee.
Managers of Catholic schools in the Glasgow Archdiocese establish St Kentigern's Hostel in the former seminary building in Partickhill as a residence for Catholic men preparing for teaching at Training Colleges/University. Regulations for Education, Training and Certification of Teachers for Various Grades of Schools (Primary, secondary or Special) require completion of an approved course of secondary education and professional training of minimum two years at a Teacher Training College or a Scottish university.
Beatification of Julie Billiart.

1907 Pupil-Teacher system ends.
Glasgow Provincial Committee acquire site for centralising teacher training at Jordanhill.

1908 Beatification of Madeleine Sophie Barat.

1912 Notre Dame Institute acquire Clerkhill.

1914–18 The Great War.

1915 Main building at Jordanhill completed.

1918 Education (Scotland) Act.
Craiglockhart Hydropathic used as a hospital for shell-shocked British Army officers. Wilfrid Owen and Siegfried Sassoon among the patients.

1920 National Committee for teacher training replaces the Provincial Committees.

1921 Church promulgates regulations for teacher training of men and women.
No woman training in Scotland would be eligible for employment in a Catholic school who has trained in whole or in part in any but Catholic centres and Training Colleges.
Jordanhill College opens. Three hundred at College School.

1922 Donald Mackintosh appointed Archbishop of Glasgow.

	Sub-Committee of Religious Inspectors forms to supervise the religious training of male prospective teachers.
1924	Graduation at a University required for all male teachers, except in Art, Music, Physical Education and Technical Education.
	Hierarchy wishes a Training College for men to be established in Glasgow to be managed by a community of priests.
	National Committee for teacher training replaces Provincial Committees.
	Colleges for men and women at Aberdeen, St Andrews, Glasgow and Edinburgh; College of Hygiene, for men and women, at Dunfermline; and three Colleges for women only: Craiglockhart, Notre Dame and Episcopal College. Principals from members of the Religious communities.
1926	Degree or Central Institution Diploma essential for all male entrants into teaching.
	Minimum academic qualification for women is now Group Leaving Certificate.
	General Strike.
	Death of J. S. Phillimore.
1928	Beatification of John Ogilivie.
1930	The Great Depression. Cuts in Social Services.
	Catholic University Chaplaincy opens at 53 Southpark Avenue, Glasgow.
1939	Outbreak of World War II.
	Threat of evacuation. St Charles's College (London) evacuate to Berkshire.
	Society of the Sacred Heart houses at Roehampton and Saint Charles Square suffer severely from enemy action.
1940	Mother House of the Notre Dame Institute at Namur destroyed, but community safe.
1941	Sister Magdalene of Saint Bernard becomes Principal.
1944	Beveridge Report lays foundation of the Welfare State.
1945	Hiroshima. World War II ends.
	General Election. Labour Government under Attlee brought to power.
	Rev. William E. Brown, first Catholic chaplain of Glasgow University, retires. Education Act. Free Primary, Secondary and Further Education.

Junior Colleges for 16–18 year-olds.
Milk and meals to be provided in all schools.
Marriage becomes no bar to women teachers.
Occupation of Europe. Nuremberg trials.

1946 Report of the Advisory Council on Education in Scotland. Education Act.
Free Primary, Secondary and Further Education.
Milk and meals to be provided in all schools. Marriage no bar to women teachers.
Saint Peter's seminary, Bearsden destroyed by fire.

1947 Raising of School Leaver age to fifteen. Emergency Recruitment Scheme introduced.

1948 Restoration of the Scottish Hierarchy.
Cistercian Abbey founded at Nunraw.

1950 Proclamation of the Dogma of the Assumption of Our Lady into Heaven.
Encyclical *Humanæ Generis.*

1952 Special Recruitment Scheme introduced. Turnbull Hall opens.

1957 Treaty of Rome.

1958 Teacher (Training Authorities) (Scotland) Regulations 1958.
Training Colleges, renamed Colleges of Education, to be responsible for shortened and In-Service courses. Boards of Studies and Students Representative Councils to be set up. Dowanhill overcrowded. Archbishop Campbell is offered the site of St Peter's Bearsden for a new building to house five hundred.
Election of Pope John XXIII.

1959 Second Vatican Council called.

1960 Gillespie, Kidd and Coia appointed architects of new Catholic College of Education in Bearsden.

1961 Glasgow teachers take strike action for the first time, in opposition to the Emergency Training Scheme and to the employment of uncertificated teachers.
Second Vatican Council opens.
Wheatley Report on *The Teaching Profession in Scotland.*
Brunton Report, *From School to Further Education.*

1963 Assassination of President John F. Kennedy.

1964 Robbins Report on Higher Education.
Third College for Catholic students to be established.
Second Vatican Council ends.
Colleges at Ayr, Falkirk and Callendar Park established.

Power to award Teaching Certificates removed from the Secretary of State and given to Colleges of Education.

Sister Francis Xavier (Ellen Henry) becomes Principal at Notre Dame.

Education Authorities to re-organise secondary schools along comprehensive lines.

1965 Teachers' Certification (Scotland) Act sets up the General Teaching Council.

1966 Dowanhill to become the nucleus of a third Catholic College.

Beginning of the 'Cultural Revolution' in China by Mao Zedong.

1967 New bulding at Bearsden opens; Dowanhill to remain in use.

Teachers' (Colleges of Education) (Scotland) Regulations 1967.

Male students admitted to the three-year course in Primary Education. Students no longer required to live in residence.

Further training of teachers in service a statutory responsibility of Colleges of Education. National Council for In-Service Training instituted.

1968 Diploma in Music introduced. Course (non-denominational) extended over three sessions and leading to both Primary and Secondary qualification. In-Service courses also non-denominational.

Official Opening of College at Bearsden by Lord Wheatley.

Special Recruitment Scheme.

Assassination of Robert Kennedy.

USSR (Brezhnev President) invades Czechoslovakia.

Trouble in Derry.

Humanae Vitae – crisis of authority in the Church.

1969 Dowanhill to take overflow from Bearsden

Notre Dame to take male Catholic graduates.

Negotiations for introduction of Bachelor of Education course to proceed. 500 places required at Dowanhill. Plans prepared for redevelopment of site to provide third Catholic College.

Conference at Notre Dame entitled 'Modern Studies in the Christian Context' attended by 140 teachers from throughout Scotland.

At Craiglockhart, Sisters leave their enclosure; Religious habit considered optional; Rome: Religious life should be a witness to communion in the midst of the world. Greater emphasis on the reading of the Bible and on need for an active laity.
Nixon President of USA.
War in Vietnam
Ostpolitik.
American rapport with China.

1970 Bachelor of Education Degree for Secondary Teachers - 4-year concurrent course of qualification and training – validated by Council for National Academic Awards (CNAA) introduced.

1971 In-Service Training Report: Rapid expansion taking place. Extensive programme planned for Summer Vacation; all college departments contribute.
First Residential Summer Course in Guidance.
Advanced Diploma in Religious Education introduced by Notre Dame College as In-Service exercise.
Upper Clyde work-in.
Rev. Thomas Winning becomes Auxiliary Bishop for Glasgow.

1972 Moscow Summit.
All operations in Indo-China to cease.
Watergate.
Total student population at Notre Dame 1542. Craiglockhart 300+.
Sunningdale Conference – power sharing in Northern Ireland. Ceasefire in Hanoi.
Liturgical changes. Scottish National Party win Govan.
Bloody Sunday.

1973 Britain enters the European Economic Community.
First lecturer in Guidance appointed in Notre Dame College, Glasgow.
Death of Bishop James Ward.

1974 Bachelor of Education Graduation. First award of Advanced Diploma in Religious Education.
Archbishop Winning succeeds Archbishop Scanlan.
Specialist Qualification for Teachers of Religious Education introduced.
Nixon resigns. Gerald Ford President of USA.
February General Election: Conservatives defeated.

1975	Decrease in Scottish student population. Roll of Notre Dame College 1336. Increase in In-Service Training.
	Qualifying Courses in Guidance introduced nationally in Scotland. Course in Special Education introduced at Notre Dame College, Glasgow.
	North Vietnam invades South Vietnam.
	Repressive dictatorships in Chile, Angola, USSR, China.
	Helsinki conference.
	Breschnev Doctrine.
	Détente – avoidance of war and revolution – balance within USSR.
	Margaret Thatcher Head of Conservative Party.
1976	Canonisation of John Ogilvie.
	Death of Mao, succeeded by Deng Xiaopeng; end of 'Cultural Revolution'.
	Jimmy Carter, President of the USA
	In Northern Ireland, 'Special Category' status for political prisoners.
1977	Auxiliary Bishops Renfrew and Joseph Devine appointed to Archdiocese of Glasgow.
	Pack Committee Report published.
	Election of Pope John Paul II.
1978	Sister Francis Ellen Henry retires. Sister Margaret Sheridan becomes Principal at Notre Dame.
	John Paul II visits Ireland and Poland.
	USSR invades Afghanistan.
	Referendum for Scottish Assembly.
1980	Moscow Olympics.
	Lech Wałęsa: the rise of Solidarność (Solidarity).
	End of Détente.
	Reagan President of USA.
	Murder of Archbishop Romero.
1981	St Andrew's College of Education forms from merger of Notre Dame and Craiglockhart Colleges; becomes the National Catholic College of Scotland to operate on Bearsden and Craiglockhart sites, which is concerned solely with training of men and women who are or wish to be teachers. A Sister of Notre Dame to be College Principal and a Sister of the Society of the Sacred Heart the director of Craiglockhart site. Prospective Catholic teachers required to follow the course in Religious Education.

Distance Learning courses introduced, backed by In-Service courses at bases in Edinburgh and Dundee.
Royal College of Science and Technology given university status as the University of Strathclyde.
Attempted assassination of John Paul II.
Hunger strike in Belfast; death of Bobby Sands.

1982 Heriot-Watt given University status.
Stirling University founded.

1983 Scottish Central Committee on Guidance (SCCG).
All teachers to have appropriate Guidance training.

1984 National Council for In-Service Training Report: Staff Development, Three-Tier structure, School-focused In-Service Training. National qualifications for Special Teachers of Religious Education introduced; Agreement reached between Scottish Education Department and Catholic Education Commission that H. M. Inspectors have right to inspect professional aspects of religious education in Catholic schools. The approval of teachers to posts in Catholic schools is the concern of the Hierarchy. In view of the many changes affecting Religious Education, the Commission approaches the government to discuss an amendment to the Education (Scotland) Act 1980, reaffirming the right of the local bishop to 'approve [the] religious belief and character' of any teacher to be appointed to a Catholic school. This amendment becomes part of the Self-Governing Schools etc (Scotland) Act, 1989. When the fall in student numbers reaches the tertiary level, the organisation of higher education is overhauled. The Council for National Academic Awards is wound up, St Andrew's College becomes an Associate College of the University of Glasgow.
Disaster in Bhopal, India.
Brighton Bombing.

1986 John Paul II makes the first recorded papal visit to a synagogue. 'The Jewish religion is to a certain extent intrinsic to Christianity. With it we have a relationship which we do not have with any other religion. You are our dearly beloved brothers, in a certain way our elder brothers.'

1987 Tories win July General Election.

1988 Constitutional Convention

1990 John Paul II meets Gorbachev.

	Collapse of Communism in USSR.
1992	Yeltsin: economic reforms. Soviet disintegration: Baltic republics, Chechnya demand independence.
1993	Tanks against Yeltsin's parliament. First Chechen war.
1994	Genocide in Rwanda.
1996	Grozny destroyed, Russian army defeated. Election held.
1997	Yes to Scottish Parliament Scotland Bill (Devolution).
1997	Death of Deng Xiaopeng.
1999	The University's Department of Education, Department of Adult and Continuing Education, Teaching and Learning Service, the Centre for Science Education and St Andrew's College merge to form the ninth Faculty of the University, the Faculty of Education, in which teacher education and the study of education is provided in a multidisciplinary research environment. It continues to fulfil the existing role of St Andrew's College in initial teacher education for Catholic schools, guided by a Board of Catholic Education.
	Second Chechen war.
2000	Putin President of Russia Federation.
2001	Twin Towers (World Trade Centre), New York, destroyed in terrorist attack.
	Outbreak of Foot and Mouth disease.
2003	Invasion of Iraq
2004	Ten more States join the EU. End of division of Europe.
2005	Suicide Bombings, London.
	Demobilisation of IRA; arms decommissioned.
2005	Death of John Paul II. Election of Joseph Ratzinger as Pope Benedict XVI.
	Hurricane Katrina devastates New Orleans.
	Israel withdraws from the Gaza Strip.
	Serious disruption in Iraq. Voices raised in USA against War.
	Science, Theology and Ontology Quest Conference in the Vatican.
2006	Iran resumes development of nuclear energy.
2007	Elections in Northern Ireland; Rev. Ian Paisley and Gerry Adams meet and agree to have an Executive in place by May.
	Death of Boris Yeltsin.

Ulster paramilitaries promise to lay down their arms.
Atrocities against Christians and Jews in Pakistan and Sudan.
Northern Ireland Assembly in place: Rev. Ian Paisley First Minister, Martin McGuinness Deputy.
Tony Blair resigns. Gordon Brown new Leader of Labour Party.
Alex Salmond meets the Muslim Community.
Exceptional monsoon in India, Nepal and Bangladesh.
Bee colonies dying globally.
Financial crisis: Bank of England and Government intervention.
Protests in Burma against military goverment.
Tropical storm causes thousands of deaths in Bangladesh.

2008 Election of Barack Obama as President of the United States.

2009 Global financial crisis deepens.

Appendix Five

Principals & Chaplains of Scottish Catholic Teacher Training Colleges

PRINCIPALS OF NOTRE DAME COLLEGE

Sister Mary of Saint Wilfrid (Mary Adela Lescher)	1894–1920
Sister Aimée (O'Keefe)	1920–1932
Sister Mary Gilbert (Doyle)	1932–1941
Sister Magdalene of Saint Bernard	1941–1946
Sister Mary Consuela (Rooney)	1946–1965
Sister Francis Xavier (Ellen Henry)	1965–1978
Sister Margaret Sheridan	1978–1981

PRINCIPALS OF CRAIGLOCKHART COLLEGE

Madame Pauline Smith	1919–1924
Madame Margaret Pope	1924–1930
Mother Hague	1930–1938
Mother Carton	1938–1947
Mother Blount	1948–1974
Mother Hayes	1974–1981

PRINCIPALS OF ST ANDREW'S COLLEGE OF EDUCATION

Sister Margaret Sheridan	1981–1984
Bartholomew J. McGettrick	1984–1990

CHAPLAINS AT NOTRE DAME COLLEGE

Clergy of St Peter's Parish, Partick	1894–1918
Very Rev. Monsignor Henry Forbes	1918–1923
Very Rev. Monsignor O. J. Claeys	1923–1925
Rev. Dom Augustus Kirk OSB	1925–1941

Rev. James Black (later Bishop of Paisley)	1941–1948
Rev. James Ward (later Auxiliary Bishop of Glasgow)	1948–1950
Rev. Thomas Meikleham	1950–1959
Mons. J. Gillespie	1959–1973
Rev. Charles Kane	1973–1974
Rev. Felix Beattie	1974–1976
Rev. J. Broderick	1976–1980

CHAPLAINS AT ST ANDREW'S COLLEGE

Rev. J. McKelvie	1980–1984
Rev. Noel Woods	1984–1990
Rev. J. Hughes	1990–1999

Bibliography

Abbott, W.J. (ed.) *Documents of Vatican II* (London, 1966).
Advisory Council on Education in Scotland, *Secondary Education: A Report of the Advisory Council on Education in Scotland* (London, 1947).
Anderson, R.D., *Education and Opportunity in Victorian Scotland* (Oxford, 1983).
Barrow, J.D., *Impossibility: The Limits of Science and the Science of Limits* (Oxford, 1998).
Brown, C.G., *Religion and Society in Scotland since 1707* (Edinburgh, 1997).
Carr, D., *Educating the Virtues* (London, 1991).
Chadwick, O., *Secularisation of the European Mind in the Nineteenth Century* (Cambridge, 1975).
Chardin, Teilard de, *Hymn of the Universe*, tr. (London, 1965).
Checkland, S. G., *The Upas Tree: Glasgow 1875–1975 – and after 1975–1980* (Glasgow, 1981).
Church of Scotland Department of Education, *Church, school and chaplain : the report of the Working party on Church and School* (Edinburgh [1987]).
Churches' Religious Education Drafting Group, *Proposals for a Core Syllabus in Religious education in Grant-aided Schools in Northern Ireland* (Belfast, 1991).
Cruickshank, M., *History of the Training of Teachers in Scotland* (London, 1970).
Darragh, J., *The Catholic Hierarchy of Scotland* (Glasgow, 1986).
Dawson, C., *Enquiries* (London, 1933).
Daly, G., *Creation and Redemption* (Dublin, 1988).
Einstein, A., 'Science and Religion', *Nature*, 146 (1940) 605–607.
—— and Infeld, L., *The Evolution of Physics* (Cambridge, 1938).
FitzPatrick, T. A., *Catholic Secondary Education in South West Scotland before 1972* (Aberdeen, 1986).
—— *No Mean Service* (Bearsden, 1995).

—— 'Catholic Education in Glasgow, Lanarkshire and South-West Scotland before 1872', *Innes Review*, 36 (1985) 2.
GILSON, E., *The Unity of Philosophical Experience* (London, 1938).
—— *The Terrors of the Year 2000* (Toronto, 1949).
HAWKING, S., *A Brief History of Time* (London, 1988).
HADOT, P., *Philosophy as a Way of Life* (Oxford, 1995).
HARVIE, C., *No Gods and Precious Few Heroes: Scotland 1914–1980* (Edinburgh, 1981).
HONDERICH, TED (ed.), *The Oxford Companion to Philosophy* (2nd ed., Oxford, 2005).
HUMES, W. and PATERSON, H. (eds.), *Scottish Culture and Scottish Education 1800-1980* (Edinburgh, 1983).
HUXLEY, A., *The Perennial Philosophy* (London, 1946).
JEANS, J., *The Mysterious Universe* (Cambridge, 1932).
—— *Physics and Philosophy* (Cambridge, 1946).
JOHN PAUL II, *Veritatis Splendor* (London, 1993).
KUNG, H., *Why I am still a Christian* (Edinburgh, 1987).
LANGDON, A. JOHN (ed.), *Religious education in Scottish schools* (Glasgow, 1979).
LORENZ, E. N., *The Essence of Chaos* (Washington, 1999).
LYNCH, M., *Scotland: A New History* (New Edition, London, 1992).
MCSWEENEY, B., *Roman Catholicism* (Oxford, 1980).
MARITAIN, J., *Things that are not Caesar's* (New Haven, Conn., 1943).
—— *Science and Wisdom* (London, 1954).
—— *Education at the Crossroads* (New Haven, Conn., 1971).
MOBERLEY, W., *Crisis in the University* (London, 1949).
MURDOCH, I., *Metaphysics as a guide to Morals* (London, 1992).
NICHOLS OP, A., *The Theology of Joseph Ratzinger: an Introductory Study* (Edinburgh, 1988).
ROUSSEAU, J. J., *Profession of Faith of a Savoyard Vicar*, tr. O. Schreiner (New York, 1889).
SACKS, J., *The Politics of Hope* (London, 1997).
—— *The Dignity of Difference* (London, 2002).
Sacred Congregation for Catholic Education, *The Catholic School*.
SCOTLAND, J. *History of Scottish Education* (London, 1969).
—— and FAIRWEATHER, I.C.M., *A Good Education* (Edinburgh, n.d. [1982]).
SCOTTISH EDUCATION DEPARTMENT, *Guidance in Scottish Secondary Schools* (Edinburgh, 1968).
—— *The Structure of Promoted Posts in Scottish Secondary Schools* (Edinburgh, 1971).
—— *Moral and Religious Education in Scottish Secondary Schools*. (The Millar Report) (Edinburgh, 1972).
—— *Curriculum and Assessment in Scotland: A Policy for the '90s*.

(Edinburgh, 1999).
SMOUT, T. C., *History of the Scottish People 1560–1830* (London, 1969).
S.N.D., *Sister Mary of Saint Philip 1825–1905* (London, 1920).
STANNARD, RUSSELL, *Science and Wonders* (London, 1996).
STEINER, GEORGE, *Real Presences* (London, 1989).
STORRAR, W., *Scottish Identity – A Christian Vision* (1990).
THOMPSON, W. R., *Science and Common Sense* (London, 1937).
ULLICH, R., *History of Religious Education* (London, 1968).
WARNOCK, M., *A Common Policy for Education* (Oxford, 1988).
WHITTAKER, E. T., *The Beginning and End of the World* (Oxford, 1942).
—— 'Aristotle, Newton, Einstein', *Science*, 98/2542 (1943), 249–254.
ZIND, P., *Les Nouvelles Congrégations de Frères Enseignant en France de 1800–1830* (privately published, Lyon 1969).

Also available from Mungo Books

Mungo Books is an imprint of Ovada Books devoted to publications of Scottish Catholic interest

A Cairn of Small Stones

John Watts

ISBN 1-905965-001

This is a tale of the West Highlands in the eighteenth century, told as the autobiography of a tenant farmer of North Morar. As Ian More McLellan recounts his life story we are carried through ninety dramatic years – through the risings of 1715 and 1745 and their aftermath, the famines of the '70s and '80s, the emigrations to the New World and the breaking up of the old clan society.

These form the backdrop to his own daily family life as son, husband, father and grandfather, and as a farmer who also turned his hand to droving, lead mining and sea-fishing.

An exceedingly well framed novel … [with] immense feeling for the land and its people. A scholarly work, but written by a man too informed to be patronising, too compassionate not to leave his reader with a sense of magic of [the] glen and the strength of its people.
– *The Catholic Times*

John Watts is the author of several works of history, including: *Scalan: The Forbidden College 1716–1799* (1999), *Hugh MacDonald: Highlander, Jacobite & Bishop* (2002) and *A Canticle of Love: The Story of the Franciscan Sisters of the Immaculate Conception* (2006).

Eilein na h-Òige

The Poems of Father Allan McDonald

Edited by Ronald Black

ISBN 1-901157-61-X

A priceless treasure
– *Flourish*

A very valuable mine of information on Father Allan and Catholic Gaeldom
– Abbot Mark Dilworth

The name of Father Allan McDonald (*Maighstir Ailein*), 1859–1905, is evergreen in the Gaelic-speaking islands of Uist, Barra and Eriskay. A native of Fort William, he wore himself out in the service of his parishoners at Daliburgh, and was transferred in 1894 to Eriskay, his beloved *Eilein na h-Òige* ('Isle of Youth'). Among his labours was the publication of a Gaelic hymnal which Ronald Black, the editor, has combined selections of in this volume with twenty-seven poems first published in 1965, providing a resulting body of some sixty items with an English translation, introduction and notes.

Ronald Black is Gaelic editor of *The Scotsman* and the Uist newspaper *Am Pàipear.* He has published *An Tuil: Anthology of 20th Century Scottish Gaelic Verse* (1999), *Smuaintean fo Éiseabhal* (2000) the poetry of Dòmhnall Aonghais Bhàin of South Uist, and *An Lasair: Anthology of 18th Century Scottish Gaelic Verse* (2001).

Available from Ovada Books

To Heal the Broken Hearted

The Life of Saint Charles of Mount Argus

Paul Francis Spencer CP

ISBN 978-1-905965-02-1

Anyone interested in the life of Saint Charles, this holy man, will find this book inspiring and helpful. He represents the ideal of a humble, holy and dedicated priest.
– Father Benedict Groeschel CFR

For almost thirty years Saint Charles was visited daily by hundreds of people who came to Mount Argus in Dublin to receive his blessing and to be prayed over for physical, emotional and spiritual healing.

This biography reveals Charles's own inner struggles through which he learned compassion and understanding for others. Removed from Dublin for a time 'because of his extraordinary cures', he was until the end of his life subjected to criticism and humiliation, even within his own religious community. Crippled by constant pain in his later years, he continued to devote his life to the poor, the sick and the needy.

His life exemplifies that fusion of action and contemplation which was intrinsic to his vocation as a Passionist. Following the teaching of Saint Paul of the Cross, Charles centred all his prayer and activity on the Mystery of the Cross. His life manifests his deep awareness of the profound link between the Crucified Christ and the crucified ones of our world.

Paul Francis Spencer CP, edited *Letters of Father Charles* (Passionist Publications, 1985) and translated with Martin Coffey CP *In the Heart of God: The Spiritual Teaching of Saint Paul of the Cross* (Ovada, 2008). In 1994 his work *As a Seal Upon Your Heart: The Life of Saint Paul of the Cross, Founder of the Passionists* was published with St Pauls.

Herald of Hope

Reflections on the Life & Spirit of Saint Charles of Mount Argus

ISBN 978-1-905965-01-4

Stimulating reading
– *The Tablet*

What can someone who died over a hundred years ago possibly say to us today? Saint Charles of Mount Argus died in Dublin in 1893. Can his life speak to people who live in a very different world? These reflections on Charles's life and spirit attempt to allow him to dialogue with us, to share with us his sense of what it means to be a disciple of Jesus Christ.

Contributors: Martin Coffey CP, Brian D'Arcy CP, Frank Keevins CP, Paul Francis Spencer CP, Aidan Troy CP & Ignatius Waters CP.

In the Heart of God

The Spiritual teaching of Saint Paul of the Cross

Introduction by Jean-Claude Delion CP
Translated into English by Martin Coffey CP
& Paul Francis Spencer CP

ISBN 978-1-905965-06-9

Abandon yourself into the hands of God, like a ship with neither oars nor sails, letting go of yourself totally.

A charming book, full of wisdom and good cheer … giving a sense of sanity and perspective because it places everything under the direct guidance of God and in [the] knowledge of his love. Pleasantly illustrated [with] glorious photographs.
–Joanna Bogle in *The Catholic Times*

This is a good book for priests to have in the confessional.
– Fr Tim Finigan

'Rest in the Heart of God, in a silence of faith and love.' These words of Saint Paul of the Cross are an invitation to entrust our lives into the loving hands of God, who loved us so much that he gave his only Son. For Paul, the Passion of Jesus is 'the greatest and most overwhelming work of God's love'.

Paul of the Cross is a witness to the work God's saving grace can accomplish in a heart, when disposed to welcome that grace, and willing to allow itself to be moulded by it into a living image of the Crucified.

This little book presents the main strands of his teaching. Drawn from his letters of spiritual direction, the texts it contains invite us to follow Jesus in simplicity and humility on the way of unselfish love, which is the way of the Passion.

OVADA

Ovada Books, an activity of the Passionists in Scotland and Ireland, has as its aims the promotion of Catholic faith and culture; supporting the ministry of the Passionists; and helping people to understand the Catholic Faith through publishing, retailing and other means.

Its retail outlet, *St Mungo's Bookshop*, situated in the Passionist Church of St Mungo in Glasgow, offers a unique selection of new and second-hand books; cards; music and gifts of Catholic interest.

If you would like to join our mailing list and receive our free biannual newsletter of Passionist spirituality, *Ovada*, or want further information on how you can help our work, please contact us at:

Ovada Books
Saint Mungo's Retreat
52 Parson Street
Glasgow
G4 0RX

ovadabooks.com
info@ovadabooks. com

St Mungo's Bookshop
St Mungo's Church
52 Parson Street
Glasgow
G4 0RX

stmungo.co.uk
info@stmungo.co.uk

Tel/Fax +44 (0)141 552 5523

The Passionists, a Designated Religious Charity, number sco 15760

M

Set in 11 & 10 pt Minion
designed by Robert Slimbach
for Adobe Systems Inc. in 1995